Vorwort ....

United States of America

1 Foundations

Declaration of Independence 10
The Westward Movement and the Frontier Spirit 11
Manifest Destiny 12
Difficulties in Forming a Nation 13

2 African American History

Slaves – Liberated into Misery 14
Separate but Equal 15
Rosa Parks and the Montgomery Bus Boycott 16
Little Rock Nine 17
Martin Luther King 18
Malcolm X 19
Affirmative Action 20
Situation of African Americans today 21

3 Immigration

Push and Pull Factors 22
Immigration Pattern 23
Immigration Policy 24
Illegal Immigration 25
Changing Social Structure 26

4 Multiculturalism

Native Americans 27
Hispanics 28
Muslims 29
Asians 30
Melting Pot and Salad Bowl 31
Racism, Stereotyping, Prejudices and a Culture of Fear 32

5 Security and Freedom

Nine Eleven ... 33
The Patriot Act ... 34
The NSA Scandal ... 35
Gun Control ... 36
Crime ... 37
Misuse of Power by the Police ... 38

6 Foreign Policy

From Isolationism to Interventionism ... 39
The Cold War Period ... 40
The Vietnam War – Trauma of an Invincible Nation ... 41
Reorientation after 1990 ... 42
The Bush Administration (2001–2009) ... 43
Present Challenges ... 44
US Relations to Europe ... 45

7 Economy

The Roaring Twenties and the Great Depression ... 46
Roosevelt's New Deal ... 47
The Financial Crisis in 2008 ... 48
Current Problems of the American Economy ... 49

8 Social Welfare

Help Yourself – an American Point of View ... 50
Health Care ... 51

9 Political System

Checks and Balances ... 52
How to Become President ... 53
The Election of the Year 2000 ... 54
Congress ... 55
Democrats ... 56
Republicans ... 57
The Tea Party Movement ... 58
Barack Obama ... 59
Donald Trump (since 2017) ... 60

Johannes Wahl

Abi last minute Englisch

Schnell auffrischen, was wichtig ist

Klett Lerntraining

Johannes Wahl ist Gymnasiallehrer für die Fächer Englisch, Deutsch und Geschichte in Stuttgart.

BILDNACHWEIS
Seite 15: iStockphoto Calgary, Alberta (kickstand); Seite 64: iStockphoto Calgary, Alberta (traveler1116); Seite 118: Thinkstock München (Photos.com); Seite 144: iStockphoto Calgary, Alberta (andrewgenn); Seite 145: iStockphoto Calgary, Alberta (emily2k), (TheDman), (Srabin)
Bibliografische Information der Deutschen Nationalbibliothek
Die Deutsche Nationalbibliothek verzeichnet diese Publikation in der Deutschen Nationalbibliografie; detaillierte bibliografische Daten sind im Internet über http://dnb.dnb.de abrufbar.

2. Auflage 2017
Dieses Werk folgt der neuesten Rechtschreibung und Zeichensetzung.

www.klett-lerntraining.de
Teamleitung Lernhilfen Sekundarstufe II: Christine Sämann
Konzeption: Sandra Meyer
Redaktion: Dr. Susanne Lenz, Werbach-Brunntal
Projektsteuerung: Dr. Andreas Cyffka
Innenlayout: Annette Siegel, Stuttgart
Umschlaggestaltung: Sabine Kaufmann, Stuttgart
Umschlagfoto: Thinkstock, München (Ablestock.com)
Satz: tebitron gmbh, Gerlingen
Druck: Medienhaus Plump GmbH, Rheinbreitbach
Printed in Germany.

ISBN 3-12-949318-2

10 Religion

The Puritans' Heritage ... 61
Religious Diversity ... 62
Liberal Protestantism and Conservative Fundamentalism ... 63

Great Britain

1 History of a World Power

The British Empire ... 64
The Commonwealth ... 65

2 Post-colonial Developments

Gandhi and the Independence of India ... 66
India today ... 67
South Africa ... 68
Australia ... 69
Multiculturalism in Australia, Canada and Great Britain ... 70

3 Britain and Europe

Geography is Destiny ... 71
Foreign Policy until 1949 ... 72
Brexit ... 73
British-German Relations ... 74

4 Political System

Unwritten Constitution ... 75
Monarchy ... 76
House of Commons ... 77
House of Lords ... 78
The Conservatives ... 79
The Labour Party ... 80
United Kingdom Independence Party (UKIP) ... 81
Liberal Democrats ... 82
The Electoral System ... 83
The 2017 General Election ... 84

5 United Kingdom

Devolution 85
Scottish Independence Referendum (2014) 86
Anglo-Irish Relations (until 1921) 87
The Troubles (1968–1998) 88

6 Britain's Multicultural Society

A Class-ridden Society 89
Immigration Waves 90
Structure of Britain's Multi-ethnic Society 91
Discrimination and Anger 92
London Bomb Attack 2005 93
Sleepwalking into Segregation? 94
Arranged Marriage in Asian Communities 95

7 Religion

The Church of England 96
The Free Churches (Dissenters) 97
Current Religious Issues in Britain 98

8 Social Welfare

The Welfare State 99
The National Health Service 100

9 Economy

Economic Superpower of the 19th Century 101
Decline (1945–1979) 102
Thatcherism and its Consequences 103
Challenges of the Post-Thatcher Economy 104
Structural Changes in the Last Decades 105
A Prosperous South and a Poor North 106

Literature and Film

1 The American Dream

T. C. Boyle: *The Tortilla Curtain* (Novel, 1995) 107
Arthur Miller: *Death of a Salesman* (Drama, 1949) 108

2 Challenges and Choices in an Insecure World

Arthur Miller: *The Crucible* (Drama, 1953) ... 109
Jeannette Walls: *Half Broke Horses* (Novel, 2009) ... 110
Crash (Film, 2004) ... 111
Outsourced (Film, 2006) ... 112

3 Exploring Alternative Worlds

Aldous Huxley: *Brave New World* (Novel, 1932) ... 113
George Orwell: *Nineteen Eighty-Four* (Novel, 1949) ... 114
Ray Bradbury: *Fahrenheit 451* (Novel, 1953) ... 115
Suzanne Collins: *The Hunger Games* (Trilogy, 2008–2010) ... 116
Common Features of Dystopias ... 117

4 William Shakespeare

The Globe – Shakespeare's Theatre ... 118
The Elizabethan World Picture ... 119
Romeo and Juliet (Tragedy, 1597) ... 120
Baz Luhrmann: *Romeo + Juliet* (Film, 1996) ... 121
Othello (Tragedy, 1603/04) ... 122
The Merchant of Venice (Comedy, 1596–98) ... 123
A Midsummer Night's Dream (Comedy, 1595/96) ... 124
The Interest of Young Audiences in Shakespeare ... 125

5 (Post-)Colonialism and Migration

Joseph Conrad: *An Outpost of Progress* (Short Story, 1896) ... 126
Rabbit-Proof Fence (Film, 2002) ... 127
Ngugi wa Thiong'o: *A Meeting in the Dark* (Short Story, 1974) ... 128
Salman Rushdie: *Good Advice Is Rarer than Rubies* (Short Story, 1994) ... 129

6 Asian Communities in Britain

Hanif Kureishi: *My Son the Fanatic* (Short Story, 1994) ... 130
Qaisra Shahraz: *A Pair of Jeans* (Short Story, 1988, 2004) ... 131
Bali Rai: *(Un)Arranged Marriage* (Novel, 2001) ... 132
East is East (Film, 1999) ... 133
Bend It Like Beckham (Film, 2002) ... 134

Living in a Modern World

1 Globalization

Poverty as a Global Challenge 135
Migration 136
Environmental Challenges 137
Americanization: Consequences of a Global Culture 138
English as a World Language 139

2 Technology and Media

Genetic Engineering 140
Big Data 141
Social Media 142
Power of Media Corporations 143

Skills: Analysis and Writing

1 Analyzing Non-fictional Texts

Cartoons 144
Graphs and Charts 145
Non-fictional Texts 146

2 Analyzing Fictional Texts

Setting 147
Structure of a Classical Drama 148
Ending 149
Characterization 150
Stylistic Devices 151
Narrative Perspective 152

3 Different Writing Strategies

Letter to the Editor 153
Interior Monologue 154
Dialogue 155
Speech 156
Comparing Characters, Themes and Plots 157
Review 158
Mediation 159

Liebe Schülerin, lieber Schüler,

sicherlich kennen Sie diese Situation: Es ist kurz vor der Klausur und die Zeit wird knapp. Sie schreiben sogar mehrere Klausuren innerhalb weniger Tage und können unmöglich nochmals Ihre kompletten Mitschriften oder das Schulbuch durcharbeiten. Vielleicht stellen Sie auch fest, dass Ihre Mitschriften Lücken haben – und das ist so ziemlich das Letzte, was Sie *last minute* gebrauchen können!

Keine Sorge, mit *Abi last minute – Englisch* sind Sie auf der sicheren Seite:

- In **150 prüfungsrelevanten Begriffen** wiederholen Sie kurz und knapp, was Sie in der Klausur bzw. der Abiturprüfung wissen müssen. 150 Lernbegriffe = 150 gut gepackte Wissenspakete für Ihren Weg zum Abitur.

- Die Begriffe sind thematisch zusammengefasst, sodass Sie ganz gezielt das Thema in Angriff nehmen können, das in der Klausur abgefragt wird.

- Vor dem Abitur können Sie natürlich das ganze Buch durcharbeiten und so optimal vorbereitet in die Prüfung gehen.

Abi last minute - kurz und knapp für kurz vor knapp!

Eine erfolgreiche Oberstufenzeit und alles Gute für die Abiturprüfung wünscht Ihnen

Ihre Redaktion Klett Lerntraining

Declaration of Independence

- British taxation of the American colonists (Sugar Act 1764, Stamp Act 1765, Townshend Duties 1767).

- As the American colonists were not represented in the British Parliament, they thought it was unfair to be taxed.

- Protests escalated (Boston Massacre 1770) and led to the famous Boston Tea Party (1773).

- The American War of Independence began in 1775 with the Battle of Lexington and Concord.

- On July 4th, 1776, the representatives of the thirteen United States of America signed the so-called Declaration of Independence. Among others, the following rights and principles are stated:
  - It is legitimate "to alter or to abolish a destructive government."
  - All men are created equal, and "endowed by their Creator with certain unalienable rights", among these are **life, liberty** and the **pursuit of happiness.**

- The Revolutionary War (1775–1783) ended with the Treaty of Paris, which confirmed the new nation's complete separation from the British Empire.

The Westward Movement and the Frontier Spirit

- Until 1783, the USA consisted of the original 13 states along the East Coast only.
- It took decades throughout the 19th century to expand the American territory further west, in the process of which new lands were conquered or bought from England, Spain and France.
- For many immigrants, "going west" was associated with
  - economic opportunities, e.g. land ownership,
  - freedom,
  - escaping the overcrowded cities caused by the constant influx of people from overseas.
- The frontier – the line between civilization and wilderness – was moved forward by individual trappers, followed by the mass of farmers and ranchers who established social and political communities based on democratic autonomy.
- Living at the frontier was extremely hard and dangerous. Although often ideologically romanticized, the frontier experience has shaped American values until today:
  - the idea that everyone is the master of his own destiny,
  - self-reliance and independence in the absence of governmental help,
  - individualism,
  - mobility,
  - pioneer spirit.

Manifest Destiny

- Widespread belief of the Puritan settlers that it was America's **mission** to build an ideal religious, social and political order.

- Tied to the biblical tradition of "the promised land" or "new Canaan".

- In 1845, the Democratic leader and influential editor John L. O'Sullivan coined the phrase "Manifest Destiny", trying to explain and justify the young nation's thirst for expansion. Not only for him
  - it was obvious ("manifest") that Americans were **God's chosen people**.
  - For the development of liberty and democracy, Providence had given them the right to spread over the whole continent.

- In the 19th century "Manifest Destiny" justified the conquest of new territories and the displacement or killing of Native Americans.

- Until today it is the ideological basis for America's self-perception with respect to:
  - its right (or even duty) to spread its ideals all over the world,
  - its ongoing fight for liberty and democracy.

Difficulties in Forming a Nation

- Despite the common interests against the British, there was a big difference between the Northern and Southern states of the US:
  - The Northern states had been settled by low and middle-class Puritans. Their economy needed highly skilled workers in the take-off period of the industrialization.
  - The agricultural South had been dominated by a planters' aristocracy, highly dependent on slaves in the cotton fields.
- With Abraham Lincoln's presidency, the Southern states feared that their interests would not be taken account for any longer, i.e. that slavery might be abolished. So they founded a separate state: the **Confederate States of America.**
- It is widely believed that Lincoln waged the Civil War (1861–1865) in order to free the slaves. However, for him it was rather a question of national unity.
- Emancipation Proclamation (1863): Only to weaken the Southern states, in the second half of the war Lincoln finally declared all slaves to be free.
- "Reconstruction Period": Northern control of politics and the army in the rebellious states until 1877. For decades the relation between North and South remained tense.
- Even today there are differences in mentality and lifestyle.

Slaves – Liberated into Misery

- Between 1619 and 1808 African slaves were brought to America as cheap labour. By 1860 there lived 3.5 million slaves in the Southern states.

- The rural Southern states with their cotton and tobacco plantations were part of the triangular trade between Britain, Africa and the New World.

- Slaves were not considered as human beings:
  - they were sold on slave-markets, families were torn apart,
  - slave owners used to beat slaves to death and raped black women.

- The abolitionists (an anti-slavery movement) in the North helped slaves to escape from their destiny. With her novel *Uncle Tom's Cabin* (1852) Harriet Beecher Stowe aroused many people's hearts.

- With President Abraham Lincoln's **Emancipation Proclamation** (1863) slavery was forbidden.

- Most slaves were liberated into misery. Often they stayed on the same plantations and had to work as before for very little money. Segregation and discrimination of Blacks in the South continued after the Civil War.

- "White backlash": The Ku Klux Klan terrorized black (and white) people who were in favour of black emancipation.

Separate but Equal

- Federal laws stood in sharp contrast to the Southern states' legislation.

- 14th Amendment (1868): Full citizenship to black Americans; 15th Amendment (1870): All male citizens of the US got the right to vote.

- On state level the so-called **Jim Crow laws** (Jim Crow is a contemptuous nickname for all black Americans) were passed, excluding Blacks from public institutions (schools, buses, parks etc). Poll taxes and literacy tests practically took away the ability of political participation.

- In 1896, the Supreme Court confirmed that state segregation laws did not violate the 14th Amendment, as long as there were separate similar facilities for black people.

- The Supreme Court's doctrine "separate but equal" did not match with reality:
  - Black schools were poorly equipped with desks, books etc compared to white ones.
  - Toilets, drinking fountains and areas assigned to black Americans were not as nice as those assigned to Whites.

Segregated facilities

Rosa Parks and the Montgomery Bus Boycott

- On December 1, 1955, Rosa Parks caused a revolution just by taking a seat in a bus.
- Buses in Montgomery, Alabama, were segregated:
  - front rows were reserved for Whites,
  - back rows for Blacks.
  - Blacks had to stand up for Whites if the white section was full.
  - Blacks had to buy tickets from the bus driver and get out again to re-enter the bus at the back; often drivers did not wait for them.
- Rosa Parks sat in the first row of the "coloured section", when the bus driver demanded her to leave the seat for a white person.
- She resisted because she was tired after a long working day (not as a political statement against segregation) and was arrested.
- Martin Luther King and other civil rights activists organized a bus boycott of the 42000 black citizens. For a year
  - black taxi drivers transported fellow Blacks for 10 cents,
  - carpools with organized stops were used by Blacks to get to work.
- On November 13, 1956, the Supreme Court decided that segregation on buses was unconstitutional.
- Beginning of the non-violent **Civil Rights Movement**.

Little Rock Nine

- History-making decision of the Supreme Court: Brown vs Board of Education (1954): Segregated schools are against the Constitution.
- Rejection of the long-held doctrine "Separate but equal".
- September 1957: Nine African American students ("Little Rock Nine") enrolled in Central High School, a previously all-white school, in Little Rock, Arkansas.
- Crowds of angry white racists, supported by the Arkansan governor who deployed the National Guard in front of the school blocked the entrance on the first few school days.
- On September 24, 1957, President Dwight D. Eisenhower sent in US Army soldiers to help the black students. Each of the nine students got a soldier as bodyguard.
- Nevertheless, the black students had to suffer from continuous physical and verbal abuse, i.e. racist comments, being called names. Melba Pattillo had acid thrown into her eyes.
- Final attempt of Arkansas's governor to prevent the nine students from finishing their education: closing the school ("The Lost Year"). However, in the end three of them graduated from Central High.

Martin Luther King

- Baptist minister and the undisputed leader of the Civil Rights Movement.
- In his non-violent strategy he was deeply influenced by Gandhi's fight for Indian Independence and his Christian faith.
- King became nation-wide known as organizer of the Montgomery bus boycott (1955).
- Stages of his campaign with the means of **civil disobedience** were:
  - protests in Birmingham, Alabama (1963), which attracted national media coverage of the brutal police response,
  - the March on Washington where he held his famous speech **"I have a dream"** (1963),
  - march from Selma to Montgomery (1965).
- King was arrested 29 times.
- Due to his influence President Johnson signed
  - the **Civil Rights Act** (1964),
  - the **Voting Rights Act** (1965).
- In 1964, King received the Nobel Peace Prize for combating racial inequality through non-violence.
- He was assassinated in Memphis, Tennessee (1968).

Malcolm X

- Born as Malcolm Little, he dropped his surname later as it was given to his family in times of slavery.

- **Muslim minister**, associated with the organization "Nation of Islam".

- In his years under the influence of the Nation of Islam, Malcolm X believed in
  - black supremacy,
  - a separate nation of Blacks within the USA; he was against integration.
  - He condemned the white race as devils.
  - He rejected King's non-violent strategy as inefficient and advocated that Blacks should protect themselves "by any means necessary", including **violence**.

- Disillusionment and separation from the Nation of Islam (1964).

- Despite harsh criticism, Malcolm X has been described as one of the greatest and most influential African Americans in history:
  - He is credited with raising the self-esteem of black Americans and reconnecting them with their African heritage.
  - He is considered largely responsible for the spread of Islam in the black community in the United States.
  - Many African Americans, especially those who lived in bad conditions in the cities, felt that Malcolm X articulated their complaints concerning inequality better than the mainstream Civil Rights Movement did.

- Murdered by three members of the Nation of Islam (1965).

Affirmative Action

- Controversial programme introduced in the 1960s by President Kennedy to take active steps in eliminating (racial) discrimination in employment and education.

- Measures in this context have been:
  - **Equal Opportunity and Employment Act** (1972): preferential treatment of minorities with equal qualifications,
  - anonymous applications,
  - "busing" in order to provide equal opportunities in education: some black children in certain areas were brought to "white" schools and vice versa.

- Affirmative Action has also been used to promote the position of women and disabled persons (fighting discrimination on the basis of gender or disabilities).

- Advocators believe:
  - It compensates past discrimination,
  - opens doors for historically excluded groups in workplace settings and higher education,
  - has helped to create a greater diversity in institutions and companies necessary in a global world.

- Opponents argue:
  - Affirmative Action has a negative bias towards Asian Americans and white men,
  - it only reverses discrimination,
  - favours only middle and upper class minority people,
  - provokes envy and hostility towards the preferred groups.

Situation of African Americans today

- The overall picture of African Americans today is quite **ambiguous.**

- Obviously the situation of African Americans has been improved compared to the situation 50 years ago.
  - There is a black middle and upper class, which is highly educated and economically/politically successful.
  - Examples range from famous sportsmen, actors or entertainers to politicians – even in the Republican Party (e.g. Colin Powell, Condoleezza Rice),
  - most importantly: President Barack Obama.

- However, the mass of African Americans is still disadvantaged:
  - Integration of residential areas, and consequently in schooling, has failed; one third of Blacks lives in run-down ghettos.
  - 12.8 % suffer from unemployment, a higher rate than other races in the US.
  - The rate of African Americans living below the poverty line (27.2 %) is three times as high as for Whites.
  - African Americans are more likely to drop out of school without graduation.
  - Teenage pregnancy is much more common among African Americans than in the white community.
  - There is a higher infant mortality.
  - Homicide is the leading cause of death for all African American males between the ages of 15 and 34.
  - One in five of all black males in this group has a criminal record.
  - Discrimination and racism go on.

Push and Pull Factors

- Push factors drive people away from their homes, pull factors draw them into a particular country.

- Pull factors for immigration can be summed up under the concept of the **American Dream**:
  - Image of the USA as the land of the free, providing unlimited possibilities.
  - **"From rags to riches"**: If you work hard, you can make it to the top.
  - It does not matter where you come from (including social background).

- Other pull factors have been cheap land (19th century), the gold rush and family ties.

- Push factors differed from country to country:
  - famine or drought (e.g. Irish Potato Famine in the 1840s),
  - religious persecution (e.g. Puritans, pogroms against Jews),
  - political persecution (e.g. after the German Revolution of 1848),
  - war or civil war (e.g. World War II, Vietnamese refugees),
  - economic hardship (e.g. immigrants from south-eastern European countries and Mexico),
  - lack of educational prospects,
  - environmental problems (e.g. China, 21st century).

- Often it has been a combination of push and pull factors which motivated people to come to the US.

Immigration Pattern

- Immigration in the 19th century mainly from Northern and Western Europe (England, Ireland, Germany).
- Peak in 1907, mainly due to new pattern of Southern and Eastern European immigrants ("new immigration").
- Sharp drop of the immigration rate after 1920 due to lack of opportunities, restrictions on immigration and the Great Depression (1929 ff.).
- After 1965 increase of immigration from Latin America (Mexico, El Salvador, Honduras) and Asia (Vietnam, Philippines, India, China).
- 21st century
  - In 2013 there were over 41.3 million foreign born in the United States, representing 13% of the total population.
  - 29% have arrived between 2000 and 2009,
  - 10% have immigrated since 2010.

Immigration Policy

- With moderate numbers of immigrants in the 19th century, the USA practised an open-door policy to people from Europe.

- The Chinese Exclusion Act (1882, permanent since 1902) and other laws (1917), however, restricted the numbers of immigrants from Asia and the Pacific.

- **Ellis Island** in New York Harbor opened in 1892 as a checkpoint for newly arriving immigrants (equivalent to Angel Island on the west coast):
  - Immigrants with diseases were sent back,
  - literacy tests should exclude lower class people from south-eastern Europe,
  - first-class passengers and people with money were preferred, poor people could be barred from immigration.

- Johnson-Reed Immigration Act (1924) created nationality quotas based on the census of 1890, thus preferring ongoing immigration from Northern Europe.

- McCarren-Walter Act (1952) introduced quotas for previously excluded Asian nations. The Hart-Cellar Act (1965) replaced the nationality-based system with hemispheric maxima. Immigration from India, Korea, the Philippines and other Asian nations soared.

- Immigration Act of 1990 increased legal immigration to the United States by 40%.

- Immigration Responsibility Act (1996) set up income tests for those trying to bring family members to the US.

Illegal Immigration

- Since 2000 the number of illegal immigrants has risen 37%; according to official numbers, 11.4 million "undocumented" workers live in the USA (2012), others believe it could be up to 20 million people.

- Most illegal immigrants come from Mexico (56%), who cross the Rio Grande ("wetbacks") and stay in border states such as California and Texas.

- Illegal immigrants are permanently at risk of being caught by the authorities; they face a lot of problems, e.g.
  - being always on the run,
  - lack of social security,
  - bad housing conditions,
  - being exploited with extremely low wages,
  - being considered a threat to national security by conservatives.

- **Ineffective border control** despite patrols, electronic equipment and high fences. Those who are caught and sent back often try to enter the US again.

- Different political strategies to cope with the problem of illegal immigration:
  - The **Democrats** are traditionally more willing to legalize the status for those immigrants who have been in the US for quite a while.
  - With his executive action in 2014, President Obama allowed 45% of illegal immigrants to legally stay and work in the US.
  - The **Republicans** are more intolerant and propose either sending them back or creating conditions under which they volunteer to move to their home countries.

Changing Social Structure

- Immigration obviously has a great impact on American society.
- Up until the 1960s, the vast majority of the country's inhabitants were white. 50 years later it is obvious that the constant influx of immigrants has dramatically changed the structure of the population.
- Within the last ten years, the percentage of Whites has fallen from 70% to 63%. **Hispanics,** the fastest-growing ethnic group, have overtaken African Americans, comprising about 17%.

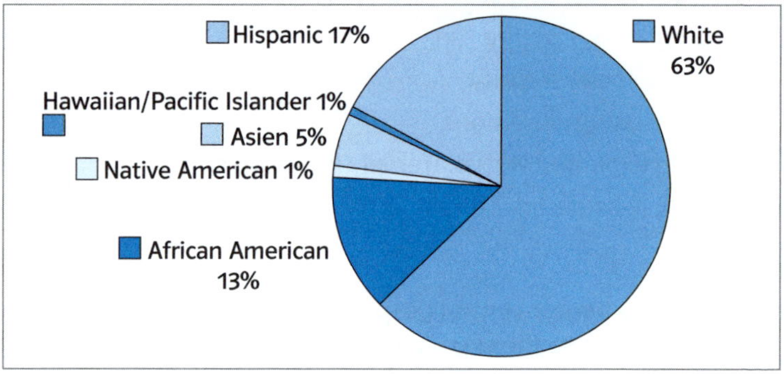

Source: US Census 2012

- At present, minorities make up one third of the US population. However, it is believed that they will constitute the majority by 2042.
- Given the current demographic pattern, Whites will only account for 47% of the population in the year 2050. The Hispanic community is projected to nearly triple to 132.8 million (29% of the whole population) until then.
- The changing social structure will have severe political consequences, as minorities tend to vote for the Democrats.

Native Americans

- Population of 2.5 million (2012); most of them live in non-reservation areas in Oklahoma, Arizona, New Mexico and Utah. 800,000 live on one of 250 reservations (e.g. Navajo reservation). Many suffer from unemployment, bad health and lack of education.

- Indian culture and religious beliefs followed the principles of
  - common, not private property,
  - no permanent settlement in favour of moving around for the best seasonal hunting opportunities,
  - no exploitation of nature or unnecessary killing of animals, as it is a sacrilege. All living beings on earth are linked to each other in a chain which must not be disturbed.

- With the frontier moving westward, Native Americans were disowned and sent to isolated reservations, most of which with poor soil and no hunting grounds.

- In the course of the 19th and 20th century, Native Americans' reactions ranged from
  - military actions (1860–1890, resistance was broken by the massacre at Wounded Knee, 1890),
  - depression, drug addiction, alcoholism, suicide,
  - spectacular forms of protest (e.g. the occupation of Alcatraz, Red Power Movement in the 1960s).

- All governmental attempts to **assimilate** Native Americans have failed.

- Since the 1970s they were granted **self-determination** in order to preserve their own culture.

Hispanics

- With approximately 54 million people the Hispanics or Spanish-speaking Americans make up the largest minority. Due to their young age, they are also the fastest-growing population group.

- Hispanics can be divided into four main groups:
  - **Hispanos** are descendants of Spanish settlers along the Mexican border. With their adoption of the English language, they are culturally well assimilated.
  - **Chicanos or Mexican Americans** comprise 64% of the Hispanic community; they often have badly paid jobs (e.g. seasonal fruit pickers). 35% of their children drop out of school.
  - **Puerto Ricans** are concentrated in New York, mostly living in bad housing conditions. Like Mexican Americans they suffer from a low level education.
  - **Cubans,** mainly political refugees after Castro's establishment of communism, tend to live in Florida. They are part of the American middle class.

- Problems:
  - Most Hispanics cannot or do not want to assimilate. The majority speaks only Spanish, which poses a serious problem to the unity of the nation.
  - Hispanics prefer to live in ethnic enclaves.
  - Hispanic households are among the poorest in the USA. 25% of them live below the poverty line.

Muslims

- The size of the rapidly growing Muslim-American population has proved difficult to measure because the US Census does not track religious affiliation. Estimates vary widely from 2 million to 7 million.
- Even though most Americans identify Islam primarily with Arabs, South Asians (Indians, Pakistani and Afghanis) constitute the fastest-growing Muslim community.
- They are mainly settled in the metropolitan areas along the two coasts. Their education and income levels mirror the general American public.
- Due to the Muslim background of the terrorist attacks on the World Trade Center on 9/11, there has been growing resentment towards Muslims (**Islamophobia**):
  - In a 2007 survey, 53% of American Muslims reported that it was more difficult to be a Muslim after the 9/11 attacks.
  - 15% complained that they had been viewed as terrorists.
  - 54% believe that the US government's anti-terrorism activities single out Muslims.
  - Anti-Muslim hate crimes have increased, ranging from discrimination and destruction of private property to violent threats and assaults, some of which resulted in deaths.
  - Turbulences in the Middle East, ongoing civil war and violence by ISIS have fuelled prejudices and bias towards Muslims in the USA.
- However, contrasting the exaggerated fear of the American public towards home-grown terrorism, a Gallup poll found in 2011 that 93% of Muslim Americans considered themselves loyal to the United States.

Asians

- With 17.3 million immigrants, Asians make up 5% of the population.
- According to the US Census (2010), they have the following ethnic origin:

Ethnic origin	Numbers (in millions)
Chinese	4.01
Filipinos	3.41
Indians	3.18
Vietnamese	1.73
Koreans	1.70
Japanese	1.34

- One in three Asians lives in California.
- Asian Americans are a **well-educated** group. Compared to other Americans, twice as many Asians have a bachelor's degree.
- Compared to other ethnic groups they are more successful in business.
- They are appreciated by the American public for their knowledge (e.g. computer sciences) and effort to integrate.

Melting Pot and Salad Bowl

- There have been different theoretical concepts to describe American society.

- The **melting-pot theory** was used in the 19th and early 20th century.
  - Figuratively it means that foreign immigrants give up their old identities, way of lives, language etc to form a new American nation.
  - This process implies assimilation.

- Though some aspects have been realized (common language, national identity), a full assimilation has never taken place:
  - A mixing of races has never been practised. Until today, interracial marriages are not very common.
  - The melting-pot theory only worked for white immigrants from North-Western Europe who had the same cultural background.
  - The "new immigrants" (after 1880) from the Mediterranean formed their own quarters (e.g. "Little Italy") in which they kept their old lifestyle and traditions.

- Today, sociologists prefer to talk of a **"salad bowl"**.
  - Every ingredient is distinguishable and valuable to the whole.
  - In a figurative sense, this means that immigrants keep their ethnic and cultural background or identities.
  - The different parts are integrated in American society which is accepted to be multicultural, diverse and pluralistic.

- Similar concepts which stress the idea of the "salad bowl" are the images of an "orchestra", a "pizza", a "mosaic" or a "quilt".

Racism, Stereotyping, Prejudices and a Culture of Fear

- Multiculturalism confronts the US with a lot of serious problems.
- Despite the successes of the Civil Rights Movement, racism – in particular towards African Americans – is by no means overcome. Beyond a façade of political correctness, there are widespread **racial prejudices**.
- Racial discrimination and economic deprivation cause anger and aggression.
- The ethnic groups often tend to seal themselves off from each other. They live in different neighbourhoods and have very little in common.
- Lack of contact is a basis for stereotyping as prejudices cannot be falsified. It also leads to insecurity which turns into fear of the unknown.
- Insufficient ability to speak English creates an additional barrier in communication.
- Some people argue that the USA is dominated by a **culture of fear**, e.g.
  - white fear of black America,
  - fear of terrorist attacks (triggered by 9/11).
- As a result, gun ownership has dramatically risen since 2001.

Nine Eleven

- On September 11, 2001, al-Qaeda terrorists launched a coordinated attack on the USA with four passenger airline flights:
  - Two planes were crashed into the Twin Towers of the World Trade Center,
  - one plane hit the Pentagon,
  - the forth one crashed into a field in Pennsylvania after other passengers had tried to overcome the hijackers.
- The United States responded to the attacks by
  - the **War on Terror**, parts of which were
  - invading Afghanistan to depose the Taliban, which had harboured al-Qaeda,
  - re-opening the War on Iraq and overthrowing its dictator Saddam Hussein,
  - establishing a detention camp in Cuba on **Guantánamo Bay** in which detainees were not entitled to a regular trial or protected by the Geneva Conventions; instead they were tortured.
- The Bush administration strengthened anti-terrorism legislation and expanded the powers of law enforcement and intelligence agencies to prevent further terrorist attacks by the
  - **Patriot Act,**
  - **Homeland Security Act.**
- 9/11 left the USA in a climate of fear.
- As a consequence, American Muslims suffered from hate crimes, negative stereotyping and suspicion of being a terrorist.
- Some people believe 9/11 to be an "inside job", a US governmental conspiracy to lure the American public into the War on Terror and to regain domestic power.

The Patriot Act

- Law passed shortly after the attacks of 9/11, comprising a set of **most controversial** measures to protect the US from further terrorist attacks:
  - Sec. 206 widens the possibility of using wiretaps without court order.
  - Sec. 213: Secret services are allowed to search a home or business without the owner's consent or knowledge.
  - Sec. 215: The FBI can seize "any tangible thing" without a warrant as long as the FBI links it to an authorized investigation.
  - Sec. 218 makes it easier to start foreign intelligence wiretaps and searches.
  - The Patriot Act has enabled the NSA to collect in-depth communication data.
  - It allows easier access to bank accounts in order to cut off the financial support of terrorist groups, and
  - indefinite detention of non-Americans.

- Critics are worried about
  - intelligence services having gained too much power,
  - the severe infringement of civil rights,
  - the possibility of misuse by the FBI, CIA and NSA,
  - the fact that security and freedom seem to be out of balance.

- Following a lack of Congressional approval, parts of the Patriot Act expired in June 2015, but have been restored in modified form by **the USA Freedom Act**. Section 215 of the law was amended to stop the American intelligence agencies from continuing their mass phone data collection programme.

The NSA Scandal

- Unknown to the American public, the National Security Agency (NSA) has collected mass communication data since 2001 in order to prevent terrorist activities.
  - Secret collection of telephone records of tens of millions US customers, using data provided by the telephone companies AT&T, Verizon and BellSouth.
  - Prism Program (since 2007): direct access to the servers of Google, Facebook, Yahoo, YouTube, Apple and Skype.
  - Collection of data has not been limited to suspects, but applied on a mass scale, affecting millions of innocent ordinary Americans.

- Practice established under the Bush administration, but secretly continued under Obama.

- Even international allied politicians, e.g. Chancellor Angela Merkel, have been spied on.

- Made public by the **whistleblower Edward Snowden**, a former employee of the NSA, in 2013.

- The NSA scandal did not only show the **total surveillance** of the American public, but also the insecurity and paranoia caused by 9/11.

Gun Control

- **2nd Amendment** to the Constitution: "[...] the right of the people to keep and bear Arms, shall not be infringed."

- Easy access to guns for self-defence and hunting.

- Statistics (2010):
  - Roughly 300 million firearms owned by civilians in the United States. Of these, about 100 million are handguns;
  - weapons in 45% of all American households;
  - about one million incidents per year in which Americans use guns to protect themselves;
  - gun ownership has risen 37% since 2001.

- Problems:
  - At the 2013 homicide rate, roughly one in every 285 Americans will be murdered in the course of their lives. 67% murders are carried out with a gun.
  - In homes with guns, the homicide of a household member is almost three times more likely to occur than in homes without guns.
  - With easy access to weapons, the risk of murderous rampages increases. The USA is the country with the most mass shootings.

- Influential lobby for unlimited gun ownership: **National Rifle Association (NRA).**

- Republicans are in favour of the 2nd Amendment, Democrats tend to strive for a reform (i.e. stricter limitations).

Crime

- Media (esp. crime series) suggest the USA to be a country of crime.
- However, crime rates have varied over time, with a sharp rise after 1963, reaching a broad peak between the 1970s and early 1990s.
- Since then, crime has declined significantly in the United States, and current crime rates are approximately the same as those of the 1960s.
- African Americans commit more crimes than other ethnic groups. Among persons arrested for homicide in 2011, 49.7% were black, 48% were white, and 2.3% were of other races.
- Overall, males, people with lower incomes, those younger than 25, and Non-whites are more likely to become victims of crime.
- Despite declining figures, crime rates in the USA are higher than in other countries:
  - The homicide rate is five times higher than in Central Europe.
  - The risk of being raped is three times higher than in Germany.

Misuse of Power by the Police

- The American police have a very bad reputation of being brutal and racially biased:
  - In 1991 Rodney King was arrested and beaten by officers of the Los Angeles Police. The four white law enforcement officers were acquitted.
  - On August 9, 2014, **Michael Brown**, an 18-year-old unarmed African American, was shot in Ferguson, Missouri. The white officer was cleared of all charges.
  - In 2015, as many black Americans as never before were – unnecessarily, presumably on account of racist motives – killed by police authorities (e.g. Freddie Gray).

- Black America is alarmed about the racist actions of the authorities. Unwilling to tolerate these actions any longer, African Americans' reactions include
  - peaceful protests,
  - race riots,
  - social unrest.

From Isolationism to Interventionism

- Age of isolationism: Monroe Doctrine (1823) established isolationism in foreign policy for most parts of the 19th century.

- Rise to world power (1890–1945):
  - dollar imperialism and overseas expansion in the Pacific;
  - the USA engages in World War I (1917);
  - since then more or less interventionist policy;
  - entering World War II after the Japanese attack on Pearl Harbor (1941); American engagement alongside Russia and its Western Allies against Nazi Germany.

- Cold War (1947–1990):
  - confrontation with communism,
  - active intervention in Germany, Korea, Cuba and Vietnam,
  - leadership of the western world.

- Global role as the only remaining superpower (after 1990):
  - worldwide military engagement in war areas (e.g. Rwanda, Yugoslavia),
  - **War on Terror** including the invasion of Afghanistan and Iraq after 2001.

- Temporary exceptions from interventionism:
  - period between the two world wars,
  - 1970s (withdrawal from Vietnam, period of self-doubt).
  - Obama seems to follow a rather isolationist course, esp. by withdrawing troops from Afghanistan and Iraq and being reluctant to get involved in Syria and the Ukraine.

The Cold War Period

- The Cold War period (1947–1990) can be divided in two main phases.

- Period of **confrontation** (1947–1962):
  - Truman Doctrine (1947) promised help against communism,
  - American containment and roll-back policy,
  - Berlin crisis (1948),
  - Korean War (1950),
  - Berlin Wall (1961).
  - The Cuban missile crisis (1962) brought the world on the brink of a third World War, when the Americans insisted on Russian missiles on Cuba be dismantled.

- Period of **détente** (1962–1990):
  - provision for direct communication between the White House and the Kremlin (red phone),
  - acceptance of the division between east and west as well as its territorial hemispheres,
  - Non-Proliferation Treaty (1968),
  - Second Cold War (1979–1983) caused by the Soviet invasion of Afghanistan and the deployment of cruise missiles in Western Europe,
  - Gorbachev's inability to keep up the arms race (cf. Reagan's Star Wars Program),
  - disarmament treaties (SALT, START, INF),
  - collapse of the Soviet Union (1991).

The Vietnam War – Trauma of an Invincible Nation

- Proxy war (1955–1975) in the Cold War period: South Vietnam was supported by the US, North Vietnam under its leader Ho Chi Minh was backed up by the Soviet Union and China.

- Aims:
  - The Americans wanted to prevent communist takeover of Vietnam which they feared might cause other countries to follow (**Domino Theory**).
  - The North Vietnamese tried to reunify Vietnam under communist rule. They viewed the conflict as a colonial war, in which they initially fought against forces from France and then America.

- Warfare:
  - The USA and the South Vietnamese forces relied on air superiority and overwhelming firepower.
  - The **guerrilla tactics** of the enemy made it difficult to distinguish between soldiers and civilians, because the Viet Cong used the villagers as cover.
  - The North Vietnamese used the secret Ho Chi Minh trail in order to infiltrate the South with troops and weapons.
  - The last American troops left Saigon in a dramatic rescue attempt in 1975.

- Consequences:
  - The Vietnam War left the United States with a trauma, because it was the first war they could not win.
  - There was harsh international criticism of the American use of Agent Orange, a bio-chemical weapon which caused severe handicaps among the Vietnamese population.
  - The American society was split on the engagement in Vietnam (cf. anti-Vietnam demonstrations).

Reorientation after 1990

- End of the **bipolar** world (Cold War period):
  - necessity of a new strategy on defence and security,
  - no need for safeguarding the integrity of NATO members against the Soviet Union anymore.
- US as the only remaining superpower strengthening its global role in a **multipolar** world by
  - stabilizing conflict-ridden regions like the Balkans,
  - fighting worldwide terror networks (e.g. al-Qaeda).
- Expansion of NATO to the East by
  - opening NATO's doors to new members in eastern Europe,
  - thus challenging Russia's influence in its traditional hemisphere.
- New focus of US foreign policy on the Pacific:
  - withdrawal of troops from Europe,
  - American demand for more European self-defence.

The Bush Administration (2001–2009)

- Burdens:
  - George W. Bush's father, President George Bush, had left the Iraqi dictator Saddam Hussein in office after the first Iraq War, following Hussein's invasion of Kuwait (1991).
  - Inspections of Iraqi nuclear programme were hindered;
  - terror attacks on 9/11.

- Political answers:
  - defining an axis of evil with so-called rogue nations, i.e. countries hostile to the USA: Iraq, Iran, North Korea;
  - new strategy of a pre-emptive war: America's right to attack before a country gets dangerous to the national security;
  - **War on Terror:** invading Afghanistan because al-Qaeda terrorists were harboured there.
  - Accusations of Iraq having weapons of mass destruction justified George W. Bush to complete his father's "mission": Saddam Hussein was overthrown; however, allegations turned out to be wrong.

- Consequences:
  - Bush attacked Iraq without any UN mandate which had a bad influence on the American-European relations. Europe was split on the question of supporting the US; Germany and France did not take part in the military operations;
  - rise of anti-Americanism in the Muslim world;
  - inability of stabilizing Iraq reminded the American public of the Vietnam War.

Present Challenges

- Dealing with legacies from the past:
  - reconciliation with the Muslim world (e.g. Obama's speech in Cairo),
  - withdrawal from unsuccessful wars in Afghanistan and Iraq,
  - killing of Osama bin Laden, the leader of the al-Qaeda terrorist network responsible for the attacks on 9/11.

- New challenges:
  - Arab Spring: Obama supported the development of democracy in Northern African countries.
  - Civil war in Syria.
  - The American retreat from Iraq caused a power vacuum in which **ISIS**, a group of extreme Islamic fundamentalists, could grow.
  - **New Cold War?** In the Ukraine crisis Russia seized parts of the country, obviously following its expansionist and aggressive political course of the 20th century.

- In contrast to the militant strategy of his Republican predecessor, Obama favoured a more diplomatic approach. Successes include:
  - normalization of American relations with Cuba after 50 years,
  - agreement with Iran on the close surveillance of its nuclear programme.

US Relations to Europe

- As a result of the American commitment in World War II and its firm position against communism at the beginning of the Cold War, the USA had a very positive image among European post-war generations.

- Europeans in the 1960s and 70s, however, developed a more critical attitude towards the US due to the following factors:
  - racial inequality in the USA,
  - authorities' brutal response to the Civil Rights Movement,
  - assassination of John F. Kennedy and Martin Luther King,
  - killing of civilians and the use of the bio-chemical weapon Agent Orange in the Vietnam War,
  - the Watergate affair (1972).

- More recently, **anti-Americanism** has risen due to
  - American lies to the public about Iraqi weapons of mass destruction,
  - torture in prisons like Abu Ghraib (Bagdad) and Guantánamo Bay,
  - American espionage on western allies (cf. NSA scandal).

- On the other hand, Americans do not understand the European reluctance in joining international missions and criticize Europe's lack of commitment in defending Western values.

- With Donald Trump's presidency, the European-American relations are in an unprecedented crisis.
  - At the NATO summit (2017) Trump did not renew America' promise of defending all other member states in case of emergency.
  - After the meeting Angela Merkel stated in a speech that the Europeans have to rely on themselves in the future.

The Roaring Twenties and the Great Depression

- The 1920s were a decade of revolutionary change:
  - economic boom triggered by Henry Ford's T-Model,
  - cheap **mass production** (e.g. radio, washing machine) by the new assembly line,
  - newly established suburbs for the well-off people,
  - higher standard of living,
  - female emancipation (e.g. flappers changed women's hairstyle and fashion),
  - modern music trends such as jazz and blues.

- Unnoticed problems:
  - unfounded expectations of an ever-lasting boom,
  - dangerous speculations at the stock market,
  - financing of most investments by loans,
  - overproduction since 1926.

- The stock market crash on Wall Street in October 1929 ("**Black Friday**") caused a worldwide economic downturn, in the USA known as the Great Depression.

Roosevelt's New Deal

- The Great Depression created **unemployment** for about 25% of Americans.

- The Republican President Hoover did too little to stop the economic crisis. He believed that
  - crises turn up once in a while and are good for the market,
  - in the American system everyone cares for himself, so the government does not interfere.

- Growing distrust of the public in the political system led to the election of the Democrat Franklyn Delano Roosevelt (FDR).

- Roosevelt's New Deal (1933–1938):
  - relief, e.g. public soup kitchens,
  - recovery by deficit spending: offering jobs to enable people to buy goods, infrastructural projects (e.g. Tennessee Valley),
  - reforms, e.g. close surveillance of banks and the stock market, anti-trust laws,
  - Social Security Act (1935).

- Results:
  - In psychological terms, the New Deal gave the people hope again and prevented a major political crisis.
  - Economically of **mediocre impact**; it wasn't until after 1939 when World War II with its military industry helped America get back on its feet.
  - The governmental interference in economy and society led to unfounded accusations of Roosevelt being a socialist.

The Financial Crisis in 2008

- Triggered by the burst of a housing bubble, home prices fell dramatically, which led to mortgage delinquencies and the devaluation of housing-related securities.

- The 2008 financial crisis is considered by many economists to have been the worst crisis since the Great Depression of the 1930s.

- The public demand for money threatened the collapse of large financial institutions whose existence was essential to the complete economic system.

- **Dramatic bailout:**
  - In order to stabilize the financial system, billions of dollars had to be invested by the government.
  - The car manufacturer General Motors was partly nationalized to ensure its recovery after bankruptcy.

- Due to the similarities with the Great Depression and the New Deal, Obama has been called the "new Roosevelt".

Current Problems of the American Economy

- Only slow recovery from the 2008 financial crisis. Unemployment rate is still at 5.3% (2015) compared to 3.9% in 2000.
- Hunger for energy:
  - The USA consumes more energy than any other country.
  - In the past, the US has been highly dependent on other countries' oil (55% of mineral oil is imported). The new technology of fracking however allows the USA to produce its own gas.
  - Obama has set a 20% renewable energy target (solar, wind) by 2020.
- Loss of menial jobs: Due to global competition the US has lost a lot of its low-skilled jobs in production, which is particularly difficult for the Manufacturing Belt. Today only 19% of the workforce is employed in industry.
- 13.6% of the population lives below the poverty line.
- Governmental deficit: Bush's wars and Obama's bailout-programmes after 2008 caused a $18.1 trillion deficit (102% of GDP) which threatens the creditworthiness of the United States.
- Growing trade deficit, caused by a strong dollar and cheap imports from Asia.
- Environmental problems.

Help Yourself – an American Point of View

- The idea of **self-reliance** is based upon
  - the frontier spirit: Health and well-being are considered a private matter so that dependence on others or governmental help is rejected;
  - the Calvinist ideology: Material success is a visible sign of God's grace which means that you should work hard to reach a better life. The poor and jobless are to be blamed for their own failures.

- Consequence: no development of a genuine welfare state (in contrast to all other countries in the Western world).

- Rudimentary elements are:
  - Social Security Act (1935).
  - Unemployment benefits are paid for 26 weeks by the individual states.

- Other welfare programmes include
  - Medicaid as a health-care programme for the poor,
  - assistance for needy families,
  - nutrition assistance (formerly: "Food Stamp Program") which provides food-purchasing help to no- and low-income people,
  - free school meals,
  - housing projects.

Health Care

- Health costs have risen dramatically over the last few decades so that not all Americans have been able to afford a health insurance. Even with insurance cover, Americans have to pay about 14% of all costs out of their own pocket.
- Most people rely on employment-based private health plans (however, small companies do not offer that!).
- Governmental health care programmes:
  - Medicare (for the elderly and for disabled people),
  - Medicaid (for the poor).
- Obama's health care reform (2014):
  - The **Affordable Care Act** (ACA) made millions of Americans eligible for Medicaid in states which opted for expanding this system.
  - Alternatives are health insurance marketplaces at which people can purchase coverage on their own.
  - Tax credits are available for wealthier people.
- 30 million Americans still have no coverage in case of medical need. Minorities and people with poor income or bad health are predominant among the uninsured.
- Controversial views on the government's funding of a health care system:
  - Democrats have a long tradition of fighting for the needs of the poor and the middle class.
  - Republicans do not only fear the costs of such a system, but rather believe in the idea of self-reliance and individual care. They have even blamed Obama for being socialist.

Checks and Balances

- Political power is divided in three different branches of government which control each other: executive, legislative and judicial.

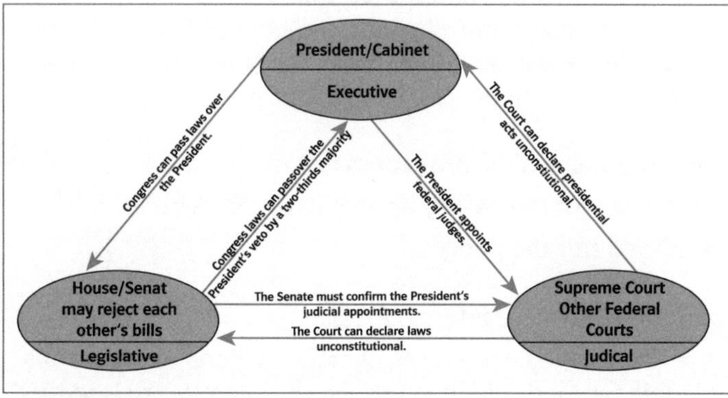

Klett Abiturwissen, Englisch Landeskunde GB / USA, Stuttgart 2009, p. 26

The separation of powers

- Problems:
  - In practice, the power of the president has been increased as a consequence of America's global engagement.
  - Some presidents (Nixon, Reagan, George W. Bush) have dominated Congress. Others, including Obama, have rather been blocked in their aims.
  - The Supreme Court has developed into a policy-making body. For this reason, presidents tend to nominate justices from their own party who are not necessarily impartial. They are appointed for the rest of their lives.
  - Decisions of the nine judges of the Supreme Court do not need to be unanimous. Frequent sentences with a close majority of 5 to 4 raise questions about the Court's interpretation of the Constitution.

How to Become President

- Campaigns usually begin one and a half years before Election Day.
- **Money** plays an important role. Candidates have to finance their own campaigns throughout primary elections (of registered voters) and conventions/caucuses (of party members).
- The National Party Conventions of the Republicans and Democrats finally choose their candidate for presidency.
- The presidential elections always take place on the Tuesday following the first Monday in November.
- The American president is elected in an **indirect** way:
  - On Election Day the people cast their votes not for the candidate, but for **electors** chosen by the candidate's party.
  - State-level decisions: The party who wins more votes in a particular state gets all its electors. All votes for the opposing party are lost.
  - Some states are more important: Depending on population size, states have 3 (Wyoming) or up to 55 (California) electors. A president needs 270 electors to win.
  - The electors who have promised to vote for their party's candidate come together in the **Electoral College** and elect the president.

The Election of the Year 2000

- The 2000 elections revealed the peculiarities of the indirect voting system for the American president and the interaction of the three branches.

- In one of the closest elections in American history George W. Bush (Republican) became the 43rd President, defeating the former Vice-President Al Gore (Democrat).

- Although Bush did not win the **popular vote**, he had the majority of electors behind him.

	Votes	Percentage	Electors
George W. Bush	50,461,092	47.9%	271
Al Gore	50,994,086	48.4%	267

- The final outcome of the election depended on the crucial state of Florida in which Bush had won by a narrow margin of **537 votes** (less than 0.01%).

- Final 5 to 4 decision of the Supreme Court to stop recounts. The majority of the Supreme Court judges had been brought into office by Republican presidents so that their objectivity in this case has been questioned ever since.

- Contradictions between the popular vote and the numbers of electors are seldom. However, in the last presidential elections in 2016 it happened again for the fifth time in U.S. history.
  - Although Hillary Clinton won 48.18% of the popular vote, she did not win the majority of the electors.
  - Donald Trump had only 46.09% of the popular vote. Nevertheless he had a clear majority of 304 to 227 in the Electoral Vote and became president.

Congress

- **Legislative branch**, consisting of the Senate and the House of Representatives.

- The **Senate**
  - cares for the interests of the individual states (cf. German "Bundesrat"),
  - consists of 100 Senators, two Senators from each state.
  - Senators are in office for six years. One third of the Senate is elected every two years.

- The **House of Representatives**
  - consists of 435 members, each representing one district.
  - The entire House is elected every two years.

- Laws must be passed by both Houses of Congress. Each House has the right to propose a bill, but can also oppose a law suggested by the other. If the president vetoes a law, Congress can override the veto by a 2/3 majority in both Houses.

- The bicameral Congress
  - reflects the principle of checks and balances,
  - is the result of a historical compromise between strong individual states and the interests of the American union.

Democrats

- The Democrats tend to be **liberal** and support lower and middle class people with **social programmes**.

- In domestic affairs, they stand for
  - same-sex marriage,
  - women's right to abort,
  - female emancipation,
  - affirmative action to improve the situation of minorities,
  - tax relief for the poor,
  - pathway to citizenship for illegal immigrants,
  - expanding access to health insurance and healthcare (i.e. ObamaCare),
  - stricter gun control,
  - renewable energy,
  - the right and duty of the federal government to interfere in society and economy.

- In foreign affairs, the Democrats
  - are more reluctant to use military force,
  - favour diplomatic strategies instead of war,
  - aim at nuclear disarmament.

- The Democrats are typically voted by the poor, immigrants, minorities, women, intellectuals.

- Regional strongholds: big cities, the South.

Republicans

- The Republicans (GOP = Grand Old Party) tend to be more **conservative** in their values. They strongly believe in the responsibility of the individual.

- In domestic affairs, they stand for
  - traditional family values, i.e. they are against same-sex marriage and abortion,
  - tax cuts for business people,
  - sending illegal immigrants back home,
  - the right to carry a gun,
  - the death penalty,
  - no interference of the federal government in the economy.

- In foreign affairs, the Republicans
  - are ready to send troops abroad,
  - are for strategic nuclear weapons,
  - advocate a large military budget to guarantee a position of strength.

- The Republicans are typically voted by the upper class, WASPs (White Anglo-Saxon Protestants), farmers, people with religious background.

- Regional strongholds: rural areas across the country, e.g. the Midwest.

The Tea Party Movement

- Radical grass-roots protest movement, closely connected and with great influence on the more moderate Republican Party.
- The chosen name alludes to the famous Boston Tea Party (1773), in which the American colonists turned against the oppression of the (British) government.
- The Tea Party is furious about Obama's policies (e.g. bailout after 2008, health care reform) and even regards him as a socialist who they want to get rid of.
- Movement combines (economically) liberal and (political) conservative values.
- Main three aims:
  - individual freedom of the people,
  - restricting the federal government's power,
  - less taxes and reduction of the national debts.
- Members are predominately white males over 45, often deeply religious.

Barack Obama – First African American President (2009–2017)

- Nobel Peace Prize 2009 for his promises to strengthen international cooperation which finally resulted in:
  - reconciliation with the Arab world,
  - turning to a more diplomatic strategy in international affairs than his predecessor George W. Bush,
  - withdrawal of troops from Iraq and Afghanistan,
  - beginning to redefine the difficult relationship between the USA and Iran,
  - normalizing the American relations to Cuba.
- With massive governmental interference (i.e. money), Obama was successful in overcoming the 2008 financial crisis.
- His historical achievement is the introduction of a **health care system** in the USA.
- With his executive action, he improved the situation of millions of illegal immigrants by changing their legal status.
- Criticism:
  - Despite his promise, he did not close the prison on Guantánamo.
  - He did not stop the massive use of drones or
  - the secret collection of data (NSA scandal).

Donald Trump (since 2017)

- Trump is the first president in the history of the USA with no prior governmental or military service. He is a successful businessman, a fact which definitely shapes his view of politics.

- "America first"
  - In foreign politics he aims at strengthening America's global role. He promised to spend more on defence.
  - In his first visit to a foreign country he surprisingly chose Saudi Arabia (2017). It became clear that human rights issues were of less importance than the billion dollar deal with the US military industry.
  - At the NATO summit (2017) Trump did not renew America' promise of defending all other member states in case of emergency.
  - He plans to renegotiate international trade treaties (e.g. TPP, NAFTA) in order to gain better terms for the U.S.

- Immigration
  - Trump wants to build a nine meter high wall at the American-Mexican border for which the Mexican government should pay.
  - In order to increase national security, he put up an immigration ban on people from seven Muslim countries. However, judges have rejected this executive order as unconstitutional.

- Environmental policy
  - On June 1, 2017, Trump announced to withdraw from the Paris Climate Agreement which was signed by all countries in the world (except for Syria and Nicaragua) to reduce carbon emissions.
  - As he does not regard climate change as a threat, he focuses on fossil fuels.

- From the very first day his populist and protectionist presidency has been controversial. He is in a constant battle with the (inter) national press.

The Puritans' Heritage

- From 1620 onwards, Puritans emigrated from Britain to the New World in order to find religious and political freedom.

- Puritans brought with them:
  - the ideal of democratic self-government (cf. "Mayflower" Compact 1639),
  - tolerance,
  - social commitment,
  - ideal of a strict separation of church and state,
  - the concept that America is the "promised land" (cf. Manifest Destiny),
  - a Protestant work ethic, i.e. the ideal of being economically successful as proof of God's favour, which triggered the development of industry.

- Despite declining numbers of Protestants, America has remained a predominantly Protestant country. **WASPs** (= White Anglo Saxon Protestants) are usually well-situated and still exercise a major influence on US society and politics.

- Due to America's pious founders, today religion plays a bigger role than in other countries.

Religious Diversity

- The United States is a country with unparalleled religious diversity. Nowadays there are more than 250 religious bodies.

- The most important religious groups are:

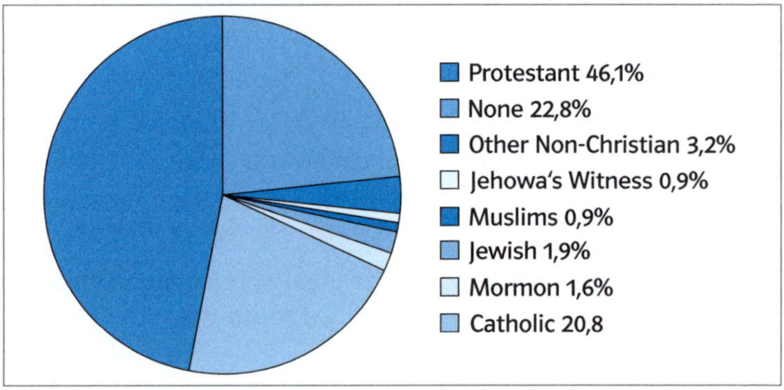

Religious affiliation 2014, Pew Center

- Long-term tendency: growing interest in conservative religious groups and small sects.

- Church affiliation reflects barriers of American multicultural society: Congregations are often socially homogeneous, speak the same language and are of the same skin colour (cf. "Black Churches"). Churches are not only places of worship, but also centres of social life.

- As churches are not publicly funded by taxes, all religious communities depend on the financial support of their members.

Liberal Protestantism and Conservative Fundamentalism

- Cultural and moral division of the country between mainline liberal Protestantism and conservative fundamentalism.

- Liberal Protestantism has engaged in
  - the Civil Rights Movement,
  - protests against the Vietnam War,
  - the Feminist Movement,
  - the fight for social and racial justice.

- Since the 1970s, this liberalism has lost supporters. Instead, there has been a religious revival of a conservative fundamentalism.

- This fundamentalism is characterized by
  - a literal interpretation of the Bible,
  - very conservative moral values,
  - a strict position against abortion, premarital sex, homosexuality and pornography,
  - the aim to teach creationism instead of Darwin's evolution theory in school.

The British Empire

- The first British Empire (17th/18th centuries) mainly consisted of the American colonies.
- At the time of the second British Empire (1783–1918/45) Britain ruled over one third of the whole world.
- Largest colonial empire in history.

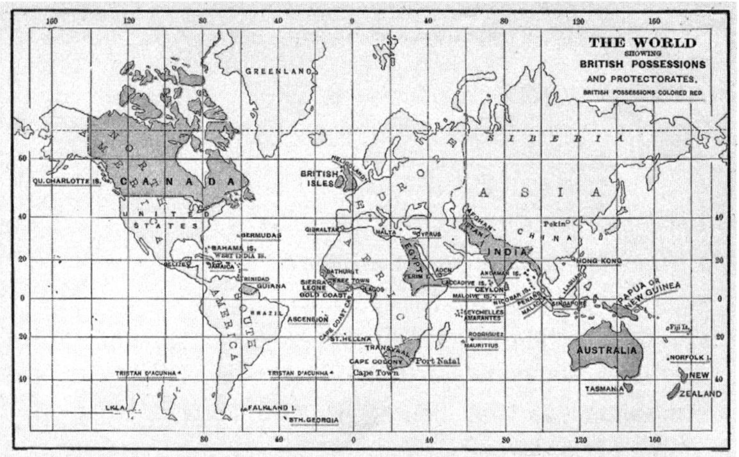

- The British justified their imperial conquests and exploitation of the colonies by their superiority.
- Similar to the American belief in their Manifest Destiny, the British thought it was their mission to spread Christian culture.

The Commonwealth

- The Commonwealth developed out of the decolonization of the British Empire after World War II.
- In contrast to the Empire, which was forced upon the colonies, the Commonwealth is a voluntary organization of **sovereign** countries.
- Most former colonies (e.g. Australia, Canada, India, Kenya, Nigeria, South Africa etc) decided to join. Countries over which Britain only had little control, such as Egypt or Iraq, as well as Burma and Ireland opted for cutting links on achieving independence.
- All 53 members recognize the British monarch as Head of the Commonwealth, irrespective of their form of government:
  - In countries like Canada and Australia, the Queen still is the constitutional monarch.
  - India, South Africa and others are republics with their own presidents as head of state.
- The Commonwealth members share
  - a common British legacy,
  - English as an official language.
- The Singapore Declaration of Commonwealth Principles and the Harare Commonwealth Declaration commit the governments of the member countries
  - to promote democracy and human rights,
  - to support the equality of women,
  - to provide access to education,
  - to fight against poverty,
  - to pursue peace and support the United Nations.

Gandhi and the Independence of India

- Rise of Indian nationalism (after 1885), politically represented by the elitist Indian National Congress which fought for home rule.

- Mahatma Gandhi turned the movement into a fight of the Indian masses. Stages of his campaign were
  - non-cooperation with the British (i.e. strikes),
  - breaking the laws by Indians' producing their own salt (which was a British monopoly).

- The British had no answer to Gandhi's strategy of **non-violent civil disobedience**. Brutal suppression (e.g. Massacre of Amritsar) only strengthened the call for independence.

- However, India was deeply divided between a Hindu majority (led by Nehru) and a Muslim minority (led by Jinnah).

- When India was finally granted independence in 1947, the country was partitioned into
  - **a Hindu India,**
  - **a Muslim Pakistan.**

- In 1948, Gandhi was assassinated by a Muslim fundamentalist.

- India had always been considered the jewel in the crown of the British Empire. As a consequence, its fight for independence triggered a much broader process of decolonization.

India today

- Economy:
  - Since the introduction of a free-market economy in 1991, India has become one of the fastest-growing economies in the world.
  - Due to its rapidly growing young population (median age: 24.9 years) and stable annual GDP growth rates of 6%, India is projected to potentially have the world's strongest economy by 2050.
  - 7 of the world's top 15 information technology outsourcing companies are based in India.
- Most populous democracy in the world.
- Challenges:
  - Despite major progress in the fight against **poverty**, India still has the world's largest concentration of people living below the poverty line of $ 1.25 per day (25% of the population – in contrast to 60% in 1981),
  - the gap between rich and poor has grown significantly,
  - fighting corruption,
  - controlling overpopulation,
  - achieving women's rights,
  - reducing growing environmental pollution,
  - eliminating terrorism,
  - ethnic and religious conflicts between Hindu and Muslims,
  - tensions with the neighbouring Muslim country Pakistan, in particular about the region of Kashmir; both countries are nuclear powers.

South Africa

- After gaining independence from the United Kingdom in 1934, the white minority (less than 20%) established an **apartheid system:**
  - institutionalized segregation between black and white,
  - Whites enjoyed the highest standard of living in all of Africa, comparable to First World Western nations,
  - the black majority remained disadvantaged by almost every standard, including income, education, housing and life expectancy. They were not allowed to vote.

- Since the 1960s, Western nations boycotted business with South Africa because of its racial policies and suppression of civil rights. International sanctions and reluctance of investors accompanied growing unrest and oppression within South Africa.

- **Nelson Mandela**
  - black leader of the African National Congress (ANC),
  - spent 27 years in prison (1962–1990),
  - peaceful transition of South Africa into a non-apartheid society together with white President de Klerk.
  - Mandela and de Klerk were jointly awarded the Nobel Peace Prize (1993).
  - Due to the black majority in the population, Mandela was elected President (1994–1999) in the first multiracial elections.

- Post-apartheid challenges:
  - extreme high rate of unemployment,
  - race riots,
  - checking AIDS which is more prevalent in South Africa than anywhere else worldwide (about 18% of the adult population are infected).

Australia

- British prison colony in the 19th century.
- The Statute of Westminster 1931 formally ended most of the constitutional links between Australia and the UK.
- However, Australia joined the Commonwealth and still accepts **Queen Elizabeth as monarch**. A referendum for a republic was turned down in 1999.
- **White Australia and the Aboriginal Australians**
  - The indigenous population, estimated to have been between 750,000 and 1,000,000 at the time European settlement began, declined drastically in the years following, mainly due to infectious diseases.
  - A government policy of "assimilation" began with the Aboriginal Protection Act 1869.
  - **"Stolen Generations" (1905–1969):** removal of about 50,000 Aboriginal children from their families and communities in order to be educated by church missions.
  - Officially justified as preventing child abuse, the forced disconnection of the young indigenous people aimed at the destruction of Aboriginal culture.
  - Legal doctrine until 1992: Australia had been terra nullius ("nobody's land") before the European occupation. Under this doctrine, Aboriginal landownership was not recognized.
  - Very late formal apology by the federal government in 2008.

Multiculturalism in Australia, Canada and Great Britain

- Australia:
  - well established integration policy,
  - migrant population has historically been mainly from a European background, with the largest source now being Asian migrants,
  - exclusion of Aboriginals ("Stolen Generations") in the past.

- Canada:
  - internationally appreciated **model of integration** since the 1970s,
  - government officially supports a "mosaic" as a model for Canadian society,
  - easy naturalization of immigrants (75%),
  - only late apology for shameful treatment of the First Nations (Native Canadians).

- In contrast to the well-working integration in Britain's former colonies, Great Britain itself faces a lot of problems:
  - immigration from ex-colonies after World War II (India, Pakistan, the Caribbean),
  - outspoken tolerant policy towards immigrants, no aim to assimilate the newcomers; instead governmental funding of (faith) schools or cultural community centres.
  - Many first-generation immigrants are well integrated, second-generation immigrants have more difficulties in finding their own identity.
  - Race riots and daily discrimination show the difficulties of that process.

Geography is Destiny

- The fact that Britain is an island set apart from the European continent has had a deep influence on mentality and politics.

- Mentality of being special (i.e. superior):
  - With the Channel as a natural sea barrier safeguarding British independence, the country has not been invaded by foreign powers since the Norman conquest 1066.
  - While continental Europe was occupied by Hitler, Britain was able to resist Nazi Germany.
  - Successful independent economy in times of European economic downturns.
  - Widespread fear of losing Britain's sovereignty (e.g. by the European Union).
  - Pride in British traditions (monarchy, the pound etc).
  - Traditionally, most British people spend their holiday in the UK or in British exclaves.
  - When British people talk about going to the continent, they usually say going to Europe, implicitly excluding themselves.

- Shaping politics:
  - For natural reasons Britain became a sea power.
  - Its naval capacity was the basis for building up the British Empire including very remote parts of the world.
  - **"Splendid isolation"**: traditional policy of non-interference in European affairs.

Foreign Policy until 1949

- For centuries British foreign policy was guided by two principles: **"balance of power"** and **"splendid isolation"**.

- The "balance of power" concept aimed at
  - a status in which no nation in Europe could dominate others,
  - securing Britain's naval supremacy,
  - guaranteeing its access to its overseas colonies.

- Principle of "splendid isolation": As long as British interests were not at stake, the British governments tried not to be involved in European conflicts and affairs.

- In the early 20th century, isolationism was given up, as rivals (Germany in particular) became too strong. Britain formed an alliance with France and Russia.

- Traditional strong links with the United States which secured US support in the two world wars.

- Reorientation after WW II due to
  - Britain's economic weakness,
  - loss of Britain's leading position in the world,
  - dissolution of the British Empire after 1947,
  - threat of the USSR in the beginning of the Cold War,
  - age of long-range weapons in which Britain's position as an island was no longer an advantage.

- Consequences:
  - NATO membership 1949,
  - in the long run: integration into Europe.

Brexit

- Britain's relation to the European Union has always been difficult.

- Late entry in 1973:
  - Britain did not join the European Union at first (1957) because of its close ties with the Commonwealth. Only after trade with its former colonies declined, Britain applied for admission.
  - French veto against the British membership.

- British concept of the EU: not a close political union, but rather a loose cooperation of independent, sovereign states.

- Britain did not adopt the Euro.

- "In-out" referendum (2016)
  - In a very close decision (51.9% to 48.1%) the British people unexpectedly decided for leaving the Union.
  - While young people opted for remaining, in particular older people voted against Europe. Lower class people were generally more in favour of leaving the EU than people with higher social status.
  - Scotland and Northern Ireland voted for remaining in the EU. As a consequence, Scotland prepares for a second referendum on Scottish independence.
  - At the core, the referendum was decided by the people's fear with respect to the growing influx of immigrants.

- After having lost the 2017 General Elections, new Prime Minister Theresa May will face serious difficulties in realizing her aim of a "hard" Brexit, e.g. cutting off all ties in a very short time.

British-German Relations

- Politically stable, but
  - the British traditionally fear a German predominance in Europe,
  - PM Margaret Thatcher was against the German reunification.

- British stereotypes of Germans:
  - Unfortunately, in particular older British people still associate modern Germany with its Nazi past. Younger generations seem to be less prejudiced.
  - Asked for famous Germans, a lot of British school children name Hitler in the first place.

- British media keep these stereotypes alive:
  - In films or comedy programmes Germans are often shown as bossy and unsympathetic.
  - Tabloids like *The Sun* or *The Mirror* frequently play with anti-German resentments of their readers and remind of World War II.

- Although Germans have a more positive view on the British than vice versa, a lot of young Germans in language classes in Britain have first-hand negative experience with British youngsters.

Unwritten Constitution

- The British constitution is not written down in a single document, but consists of codified laws (**Acts of Parliament**) and conventions (unwritten customs and rules).

- **Magna Charta** (1215)
  - guarantees personal liberties to the monarch's subjects.
  - Parliament's consent is necessary for raising taxes.

- The **Bill of Rights** (1689)
  - The monarch rules on account of the power given to him by Parliament, not by Divine Right,
  - free elections for the House of Commons,
  - freedom of speech.

- Reform Acts (1832, 1867, 1884) extended the right to vote to men of all classes. The Equal Franchise Act (1928) gave women over the age of 21 the same right.

- Unwritten conventions have evolved over time and are taken for granted by the British public.

- Unlike as in other western countries, there is no court to protect the constitution.

Monarchy

- The King/Queen **reigns,** but does not **rule.** Having no real political power, his/her role is more representative as
  - head of state of the United Kingdom,
  - head of the Commonwealth / head of state of some Commonwealth nations (e.g. Australia),
  - head of the Church of England,
  - Commander-in-Chief of the British Army.

- Limited number of rights (**royal prerogatives**): He/She
  - summons and dissolves Parliament,
  - appoints and dismisses the government,
  - gives an annual Speech from the Throne, outlining his/her government's policies (the speech, however, is written by the Prime Minister),
  - has a weekly audience with the Prime Minister,
  - has to agree to bills passed by Parliament.

- Critics argue that
  - a hereditary monarchy is outdated and incompatible with the principles of democracy,
  - the monarchy costs too much.

- Supporters point out that
  - the monarchy is an indispensable part of British tradition and history,
  - it unites the country which is torn apart by party politics,
  - it stands for continuity in times of insecurity and change,
  - its public rituals are a tourist attraction.

House of Commons

- Currently consists of 650 Members of Parliament (MPs), who represent the interests of the constituencies they come from. Of these,
  - 533 are for England,
  - 40 for Wales,
  - 59 for Scotland,
  - 18 for Northern Ireland.

- Elections for the House of Commons are held at least every five years. However, the government is free to choose a much earlier date.

- In Great Britain, the **first-past-the-post-system** is used, which usually leads to a two-party system.

- The seating arrangement reflects the traditional de facto **two-party system.**
  - Government and opposition sit opposite each other.
  - Party leaders, including the Prime Minister's Cabinet and the opposition's Shadow Cabinet, occupy the front benches.

- Tasks of the House of Commons:
  - choosing a prime minister,
  - checking and challenging the actions of the government,
  - proposing/passing of laws (acceptance of the House of Lords needed).

House of Lords

- Second (upper) chamber of Parliament.
- Members are not elected, but appointed by the Queen (see exceptions below).
- Currently consists of 816 members:
  - 702 Life peers: appointed by the Queen on account of their expertise,
  - 26 Lords Spiritual: 2 archbishops and 24 bishops of the Church of England,
  - 88 Hereditary Peers (exempted from the 1999 Act).
- With the 1999 House of Lords Act the tradition of the hereditary peers ended. Since then the House of Lords has become a **body of experts** who are not bound by party discipline.
- Tasks and rights:
  - revising bills brought up from the Commons and return it to them,
  - rejecting bills,
  - delaying bills for up to one year (except Money Bills) in order to give time for further debate on controversial issues,
  - initiating legislation.
- Reform plans propose to replace the House of Lords by an elected Senate (cf. USA), representing the different regions.

The Conservatives

- Party of the upper and middle classes, of landowners und businessmen.
- Regional strongholds: rich South, country areas.
- Aims:
  - free market without governmental interference,
  - privatization of industries run by the government,
  - reducing the national deficit,
  - strengthening individual responsibility,
  - firm foreign policy including war,
  - strong defence policy (nuclear weapons, deployment of missiles in Britain),
  - support of US policies,
  - British sovereignty within the EU, based on deep Euroscepticism,
  - restraining the power of trade unions,
  - limited immigration,
  - strict law and order policy.
- These aims were most rigidly pursued by **Margaret Thatcher** (Prime Minister 1979–1990), with dramatic implications for welfare, education and the National Health Service.

The Labour Party

- Traditionally representing industrial workers, union members and lower class people; predominantly voted by Britain's coloured population. In times of "New Labour", with its aiming at the centre of society also popular with the middle class.

- Regional strongholds: industrial areas in the North of England, Wales and Scotland, big cities.

- Alternating between socialist and free market concepts:
  - Labour PM Clemens Attley (1945–1951) nationalized industries, e.g. in the energy sector. Under his government the **welfare state** including the National Health Service was established.
  - Harold Wilson (PM 1964–1970) introduced comprehensive schools; liberal laws on divorce, abortion and homosexuality.
  - Unpopular extreme left-wing course of Labour under massive influence of the trade unions in the 1970s.
  - After a row of defeats in elections, Labour gave up its left-wing course in 1983 and began to advocate the principles of a social market economy.
  - **New Labour:** Prime Minister **Tony Blair** (1997–2007) modernized the party, pursuing a free market policy accompanied by massive investment in education and welfare.
  - The new party leader Jeremy Corbyn is rather left-wing again, advocating re-nationalization of public services and the railways. His position on the British relation to the EU is unclear (traditionally Labour is pro-European).

United Kingdom Independence Party (UKIP)

- Eurosceptic, right-wing populist party, part of the broader European radical right.
- Supporters: predominantly working-class, primarily older, white, male voters with less formal education.
- With 28% of the popular vote, UKIP won the 2014 European Election in Britain.

UK Parties	MPs in Strasbourg
UKIP	24
Labour	20
Conservatives	19

Zahlen nach: https://en.wikipedia.org/wiki/European_Parliament_election,_2014_(United_Kingdom)

- Central political goal has been "**Brexit**": Britain's exit from the European Union because of
  - fear of being governed by Brussels,
  - costs for Britain (120 billion pound).
- UKIP leader Nigel Farage called 23 June 2016 – the day of the referendum in which Britain decided to leave the EU – its "independence day".
- Additional political beliefs:
  - ending of "uncontrolled" immigration,
  - **against multiculturalism** in Britain,
  - radical penalty laws (e.g. abolition of the 1998 Human Rights Act).

Liberal Democrats

- The Liberal Democrats were formed in 1988 by a merger of the Liberal Party and the Social Democratic Party (SDP).
  - The Liberals (Whigs) had been a major political force in the 19th century, but continuously lost popularity after the 1920s.
  - The SDP had split from the Labour Party after its extreme left-wing course in the 1970s.
- Small party with little political influence.
- Regional strongholds: south-west England, Wales, North of Scotland.
- Aims:
  - expansion of **civil liberties**, in particular after Labour's anti-terror laws,
  - more direct participation of the citizens in politics,
  - free trade,
  - replacing the present first-past-the-post system by **proportional representation** (i.e. seats in Parliament in relation to the votes cast),
  - transformation of the House of Lords into an elected chamber,
  - close ties to the EU,
  - greater autonomy of Scotland, Wales and Northern Ireland.
- Lib Dems formed a coalition government with the Conservatives (2010–2015). Common decisions like the rise of fees in education harmed the party's image.
- In the 2015 General Election the Lib Dems' share of the popular vote fell from 23% in 2010 to 8%. From 57 seats in Parliament remained only eight.

The Electoral System

- Britain has a **first-past-the-post electoral system** or majority vote.
  - The candidate with the most votes in the constituency is elected.
  - The votes for the losing candidates are disregarded.
- Pros:
  - clear majorities,
  - unstable coalition governments are avoided,
  - extremist parties have no chance to win seats.
- Cons:
  - seats in parliament do not reflect the popular vote,
  - majority vote systems most often lead to a two-party system,
  - smaller parties (e.g. the Liberal Democrats) are clearly disadvantaged.
  - With 23.4% supporters of all eligible voters (2010), Prime Minister David Cameron had the smallest proportion of the registered electorate since 1832.
  - No British government since 1945 has had an absolute majority of over 50% of the votes cast.

2017 General Election

- Unusual snap election
  - New Prime Minister Theresa May ruled with a small majority only. With her call for a snap election on 8 June 2017 she wanted to extend her basis in parliament to pursue a "hard" Brexit course.
  - The most controversial issue was the parties' different plans about Britain's negotiations with the EU.
  - Whereas the Conservatives were in favour of a clear and probably painful cut, Labour aimed at a "soft" Brexit.
  - independent Scotland as a member of the European Union.
  - Seats in the House of Commons (2017)

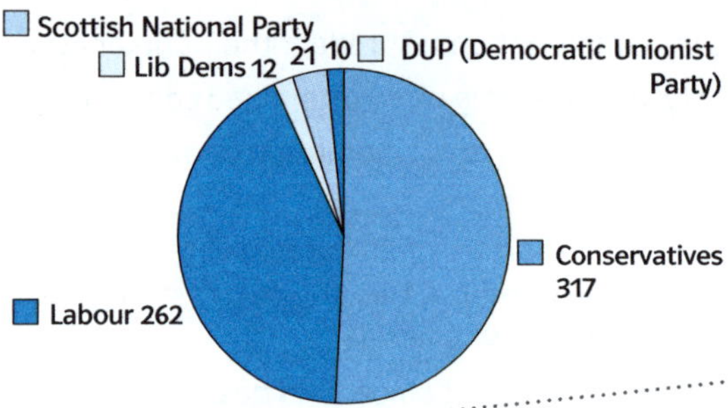

Seats in the House of Commons (2017)

- The outcome of the elections took many political experts by surprise.
  - Prime Minister Theresa May lost the elections. Her minority government will face serious difficulties.
  - Labour under Jeremy Corbyn had major gains at the expense of the Conservatives and the Scottish National Party.
  - UKIP lost its remarkable share in the popular vote (12.6% in 2015) after its main goal is about to be realized by the Conservatives. (bei Platzmangel streichen)

Devolution

- Transfer of power from the central government in London to regional assemblies in Scotland, Wales and Northern Ireland to allow more **autonomy**, following a referendum offered by PM Tony Blair in 1997.

- Northern Ireland
  - The assembly in Stormont is the earliest example of a provincial parliament.
  - "Direct rule" from London was installed again between 1972 and 2007, a time of violence between Protestants and Catholics.
  - The assembly has no legislative power concerning police, criminal justice and security.

- Wales
  - The Welsh Assembly has very limited powers (education, social services, language and environment).

- Scotland
  - The Scottish Parliament is the most powerful regional assembly, responsible for health, education, housing, transport, law and order; it is entitled to raise income tax.
  - Foreign affairs, defence and economic policy still are Westminster's prerogatives.
  - Seats in Parliament are assigned on the basis of proportional representation.

- Supporters of devolution put forward that local problems can be handled in a better way. Furthermore, people are encouraged to engage in politics.

- Critics argue that devolution creates an unnecessary, costly bureaucracy. They fear a disintegration of the UK.

Scottish Independence Referendum (2014)

- On 18 September 2014 all Scottish people were asked in a referendum: Should Scotland be an independent country?

	Votes	Of total
✓ Yes	1,617,989	44.7%
✕ No	**2,001,926**	**55.3%**

Zahlen nach: https://en.wikipedia.org/wiki/Scottish_independence_referendum,_2014

- Prominent issues raised during the referendum included
  - the future Scottish economy, which is closely linked to the UK,
  - North Sea oil (90% of the United Kingdom's North Sea oil fields are located in Scottish territorial waters),
  - which currency an independent Scotland would use (i.e. keeping the pound in a currency union with the UK?),
  - public revenues and expenditure,
  - EU membership,
  - defence (British nuclear deterrence might have been in jeopardy because the nuclear fleet is based in Scotland).

- Politicians in the UK and in the rest of Europe were glad about the outcome of the referendum, because
  - the split of the 300-year-old union might have had serious international consequences,
  - Scottish independence might have encouraged other groups in the UK/Europe in striving for a similar goal.

Anglo-Irish Relations (until 1921)

- For centuries, the Anglo-Irish relations have been difficult due to religious, cultural and economic reasons.
- In 1536 the English King Henry VIII tried to impose Reformation on Catholic Ireland (origin of the religious conflict).
- **"Ulster Plantation"** (1602): Protestant English settlers were given land in the northern parts of Ireland (origin of the Northern Irish conflict).
    - Conflict between colonizers and native Irish people, who had a different language and culture.
    - Protestant landowners constituted a new upper class, whereas most Catholics were financially underprivileged.
    - Penal laws discriminated against Catholics (until 1829).
- The victory of the Protestant William of Orange at the Battle of Boyne (1690) is still commemorated as a symbol of Protestant supremacy.
- Growing Irish nationalism in the second half of the 19th century.
- **"Easter Rising"** (1916): Irish revolt against the British rule was defeated.
- Partition of Ireland after the Irish War of Independence (1919–1921):
    - Catholic Irish Free State, later to become the **Republic of Ireland**,
    - predominantly **Protestant Northern Ireland** (Ulster), which continues to belong to Great Britain.

The Troubles (1968–1998)

- Catholic civil rights protests were met by violent Protestant resistance so that British troops had to be sent to Ireland in order to restore law and order (1968/69).

- **"Bloody Sunday"** (1972): The shooting of 13 unarmed protesters in Londonderry by British soldiers marked the beginning of three decades of bombing and assassinations. The civil war period until 1998 was marked by
  - the suspension of the Northern Irish government and "direct rule" from Westminster,
  - attempted assassination of the Prime Ministers Margaret Thatcher and John Major,
  - assassination of more than 3000 people.

- On the Catholic side, the paramilitary terrorist organization of the **Irish Republican Army** (IRA) and its political arm **Sinn Féin** (meaning "we ourselves" or "ourselves alone") fought for a united Ireland.

- Protestants rallied behind the conservative Ulster Unionist Party, the militant Ulster Defence Association and the religious Orange Order.

- In the **Belfast Agreement** (1998) all parties involved agreed to
  - the establishment of a devolved government in Northern Ireland,
  - dividing power among the formerly hostile parties,
  - disarmament.

- Repeated outbreaks of violence, mistrust and late disarmament of the IRA postponed the common devolved government until 2007. Today, the situation in Northern Ireland seems to be rather quiet and peaceful.

A Class-ridden Society

- Class distinctions and class consciousness have always played a dominant role in Britain. Three main classes can be distinguished: upper, middle and working class.

- Upper class:
  - very small group of the aristocracy and landowners,
  - ideal of the "country gentleman",
  - formerly the governing class, now stripped off their legal privileges.

- Middle class:
  - The upper middle class consists of managers, high-ranking civil servants and professionals (i.e. lawyers, doctors).
  - The lower middle class forms the biggest part of society; it consists of small business owners, non-manual white-collar workers (i.e. office workers) and skilled manual workers.

- Working class:
  - semi-skilled or unskilled manual workers, who suffer most from the decline of major industries, often depending on state benefits,
  - the unemployed, the elderly, the disabled, unsupported mothers and a lot of immigrants who are the real poor of the country.

- Preservation of class distinctions through
  - language (e.g. accent),
  - education (e.g. private schools which lead to elite universities like Oxford and Cambridge),
  - cultural preferences (newspapers, holidays etc),
  - titles (e.g. Lord).

Immigration Waves

- Before World War II, Britain had experienced comparatively little immigration except for
  - black slaves in the 18th and 19th centuries,
  - Irish people in the 19th century,
  - Jews in the first half of the 20th century.
- Mass immigration from former colonies (Commonwealth countries) due to a shortage of labour in post-war Britain.
  - 1950s: arrival of black immigrants from the West Indies, mainly from Jamaica.
  - 1960s and 1970s: immigrants from India, Pakistan and Bangladesh.
- Dramatic increase of immigrants since the 1990s.

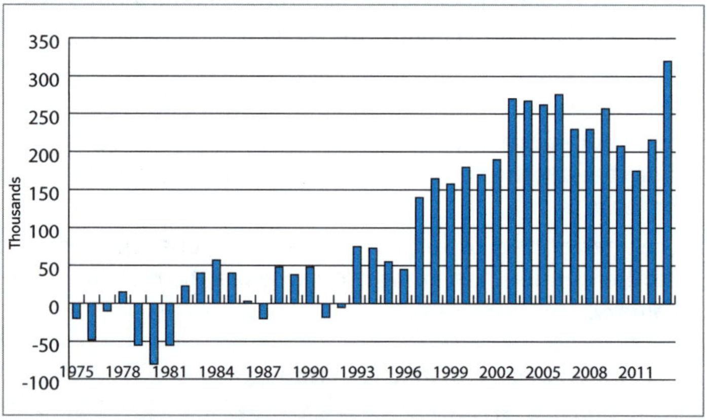

Source: migrationwatchuk.org/latest-immigration-statistics

- Most people who want to immigrate today are asylum-seekers from the world's trouble spots (e.g. the Balkans, the Middle East, East Africa).

Structure of Britain's Multi-ethnic Society

- Despite large-scale immigration, Whites still dominate British society. All non-white ethnic groups make up 14% of the population.

White		**86.0%**
Asian / Asian British		**7.5%**
among which	Indian Pakistani Bangladeshi Chinese Other Asian	2.5% 2.0% 0.8% 0.7% 1.5%
Black / Black British		**3.4%**
among which	Black Caribbean Black African Other Black	1.1% 1.8% 0.5%
Arab		**0.4%**
Other/Mixed		**2.7%**

Population structure for England and Wales according to: Census 2011, Office for National Statistics

- Asians account for more than 50% of all non-white ethnic population.
- Lately, the influx of white immigrants (i.e. from Poland or other EU countries) has begun to change British society in another direction.

Discrimination and Anger

- Many immigrants are frustrated by their economic situation, as they usually get low-paid jobs only. Ethnic minorities are much more likely to be unemployed than Whites.

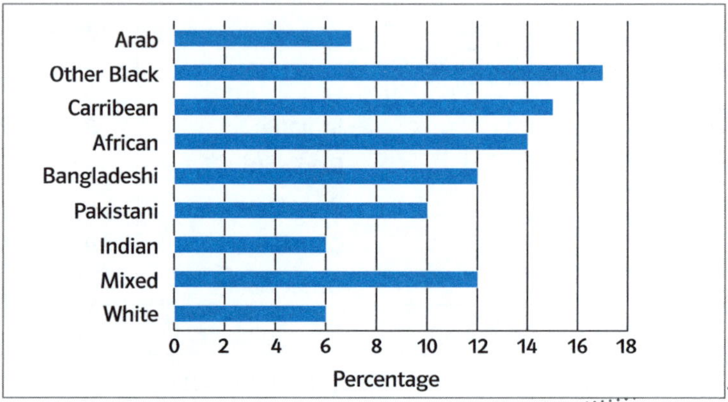

Office of National Statistics 2011

Unemployment rates by ethnicity

- Blacks and Asians are often verbally abused or even physically attacked.
  - There were reported 130,000 racially motivated crimes in England and Wales in 2010/11.
  - **"Paki-bashing"** is a fixed phrase in English.
- Difference of first- and second-generation immigrants:
  - First-generation immigrants usually tried to adapt to British culture;
  - second-generation immigrants have lost their cultural roots and do not know where they belong to. Unwilling to tolerate discrimination any longer, some turn to (Muslim) fundamentalism.
- Outburst of widespread frustration in **race riots** in 2001 and 2014.

London Bomb Attacks 2005

- On 7 July 2005, bombs exploded in a coordinated terrorist attack on three underground trains and a bus in Central London.
- 52 people were killed, more than 700 were injured.
- Three of the bombers were **British-born** sons of Pakistani immigrants, one was born in Jamaica.
- In videotapes made beforehand, the terrorists explained their motives:
  - avenging atrocities of the Western world against Muslims,
  - being devoted to al-Qaeda and its leader Osama Bin Laden,
  - warning not to support the USA and Israel any longer,
  - requesting the withdrawal of troops from Afghanistan and Iraq.
- Reactions/Consequences:
  - Similiar to the Patriot Act in the USA, the British **Terrorism Act** of 2006 imposed restrictions on civil liberties (e.g. detention without charge for 28 days).
  - Growing **Islamophobia** and a sharp rise in faith hate crimes against Muslims.
  - Most British Muslims were deeply hurt and disgusted by these attacks, especially due to the fact that the bomb site by Aldgate station had a huge surrounding Muslim and Asian community.
  - However, one in four British Muslims partly justified the attacks with the false British government foreign policy.

Sleepwalking into Segregation?

- Outspoken tolerant policy of the British government towards immigrants, i.e. no aim to assimilate the newcomers, has led to **parallel societies** of Whites and ethnic minorities.

- The ethnic minority populations are concentrated in **ghetto-like** areas in the large urban centres, in particular London.
  - 78% of Black Africans and 61% of Black Caribbeans live in London.
  - More than half of the Bangladeshis (54%) also live in Britain's capital. Other ethnic minority groups are more dispersed.
  - Pakistanis tend to live in London, Lancashire, Greater Manchester and Yorkshire.
  - 40% of Indians live in London. Major Indian communities can be found in Leicester, Wolverhampton and Slough.

- "White flight": Recent studies (2013) prove that Whites leave areas with ethnic majority population.

- In some areas there is very little contact between Whites and ethnic minorities, i.e. white children go to different schools than Asian or black children.

- Experts
  - are worried that the situation might lead to a complete alienation between Whites and ethnic minorities which usually goes along with a climate of fear and social unrest,
  - argue the government should not stress differences but cohesion, i.e. common values.

Arranged Marriage in Asian Communities

- Widespread cultural tradition in communities from the Indian subcontinent (India, Pakistan, Bangladesh) and other Muslim countries.
- Arranged marriage is to be distinguished from forced marriage.
  - In an arranged marriage the families of the two spouses choose the partners, but the future husband and wife give their consent to their families' arrangement.
  - In contrast to that, forced marriages are against the will of one or both spouses. Although prohibited by law, it is estimated that there are up to 10.000 forced marriages in the UK every year.
- Migrant youngsters are **"caught between cultures"**.
  - Most Asian youngsters do not question arranged marriage in principle.
  - For teenagers growing up in the United Kingdom, torn between the strictures of home and the freedoms of 21st century Britain, arranged marriages sometimes become forced marriages.
  - Nowadays they often choose their partners themselves but leave the arrangement (timing etc) to their families.

The Church of England

- The Church of England or Anglican Church is the **official church** of the United Kingdom, dating back to the English Reformation in which King Henry VIII separated from Rome.

- Theologically, the Anglican Church is a mixture between
  - Catholicism (monasteries, no ordination of women until 1992),
  - Protestantism (no supremacy of the Pope, service in the English language, limited number of sacraments).

- It consists of two branches:
  - Anglo-Catholics (High Church) stress the hierarchical structure of the church and the authority of the clergy.
  - Evangelicals (Low Church) focus on preaching and regard the Bible as the ultimate source of authority in matters of faith necessary for salvation.

- Despite the fact that the Anglican Church lives from its own revenues (land property, donations) and is financially not supported by the State, there is a close relation between Church and State in the UK.

- The monarch
  - is the secular "Head of the Church",
  - is officially titled "Defender of Faith",
  - appoints archbishops and bishops on the advice of the Prime Minister.

- The Archbishop of Canterbury
  - is the religious head of the Anglican Church,
  - is one of the 26 Lords Spiritual in the House of Lords.

The Free Churches (Dissenters)

- The Free Churches are Protestant Churches that rejected the English Reformation and the establishment of the Anglican Church in the 16th century.

- Main groups are Baptists, Methodists, Presbyterians, United Reformed Church and the Quakers.

- Based on the Puritans' dissent towards the Church of England, the "Nonconformist" Churches believe that
  - the Bible is the sole authority,
  - the individual is directly responsible to God,
  - the status of ministers and lay people, men and women is equal.

- The following values and attitudes of the dissenters – above all the **Puritans** – have had a strong influence on British mentality:
  - critical attitude towards governmental interference, not only in religious affairs,
  - individualism,
  - a self-controlled personality,
  - a virtuous life without idleness,
  - a Protestant work ethic.

Current Religious Issues in Britain

- **Religious diversity:**
  - Overseas immigration from Asian and Black African countries has resulted in a variety of non-Christian beliefs.
  - The number of Muslims and Sikhs has more than doubled in the last decade.

- Britain's Muslim minority (about 3 million) has been criticized for
  - threatening Salman Rushdie, the author of *The Satanic Verses* (1988), interpreted as a satire on Muslim prophets,
  - its alleged link to international terrorism (9/11, London bomb attacks),
  - its aim to spread Islamic schools and mosques over the country.

- Future of the Anglican Church:
  - decline in membership and church attendance which shows the vanishing influence of the Anglican Church,
  - deep concern about a future supply of young clergymen.

- Relation of Church and State:
  - Some people worry about the fact that non-Anglican MPs in Westminster decide crucial matters of the Church, as a result of which they are in favour of a complete separation of Church and State.
  - The future of the Lords Spiritual in the House of Lords is unclear.

- Church influence on Northern Irish politics and school education.

The Welfare State

- Until the beginning of the 20th century social welfare was considered to be a private matter in Britain. First steps followed Bismarck's model for Germany, e.g. the Old Age Pensions Act (1908) and National Insurance Act (1911).

- The Welfare State was established by war-time Prime Minister Winston Churchill and the Labour Government of Clement Attlee (1945–1951).

- Its fundamental goals are
  - social justice,
  - reducing the social gap between the classes,
  - extensive lifetime social security.

- Important parts of the welfare system:
  - **National Health Service** (NHS),
  - support for the unemployed, disabled or retired people and low-income families,
  - cheap council houses.

- Pros:
  - The welfare system meets the needs of the poor, esp. of the coloured minorities.
  - It's the responsibility of society to provide relief in times of hardship.

- Cons:
  - enormous costs,
  - discouraging people's private initiative,
  - widespread abuse of the social services.

The National Health Service

- Follows the principle that medical services are completely or largely **free of charge** for all residents.

- About 80% of the costs are funded by general taxation. Charges for prescribed drugs and dental treatments cover some of the other costs.

- Residents register on a list of a general practitioner to whom he/she has to go in case of illness.

- Problems: Funding turned out to be insufficient as costs for high-tech medicine in an ageing society exploded. Consequences were
  - long waiting lists for medical treatment,
  - lack of qualified staff in hospitals,
  - outdated medical equipment,
  - run-down hospital buildings,
  - poor performance.

- Reforms: The National Health Service Plan of the New Labour Government (2000)
  - increased spending,
  - successfully promoted efficiency,
  - expanded low-cost institutions managed by nurses for the treatment of minor illnesses and injuries.

- About 5 million (10%) Britons have an extra private health-care insurance, allowing them a free choice of doctors and medical treatment.

Economic Superpower in the 19th Century

- Britain became the leading economic power of the world due to the interplay of economic, social and political reasons.

- The **industrial revolution:**
  - Britain was the first country to introduce machines and factories,
  - British epoch-making inventions such as the "Spinning Jenny" (1764), the steam engine (1769) and the steam locomotive (1814),
  - leading sectors in the take-off of the British economy were the textile industries, coal-mining, iron and steel industries,
  - availability of natural resources (coal and iron ore) as well as cheap raw materials from the colonies (cotton, wool),
  - unlimited workforce as a result of rural depopulation,
  - triangular trade with African and American colonies,
  - enormous markets within the British Empire.

- Open society:
  - weak guild system,
  - readiness of the nobility to invest in technological innovation instead of relying on land.

- A non-interventionist government
  - favoured free trade in a capitalist system,
  - did not interfere in the economy.

- Britain lost its leading position around 1900, because the industrialization of Germany and the USA developed at a higher pace.

- In 1939, Britain still held the second rank behind the USA in terms of per capita GDP.

Decline (1945–1979)

- In the decades after World War II, in particular in the 1960s and 1970s, Britain fell economically behind the leading nations of the world. In 1986 it held the 19th rank only.

- Monetary reasons:
  - loss of British capital in the two world wars,
  - inflation rose up to 23% in 1975,
  - drastic devaluation of the British pound,
  - investment of British capital abroad.

- Political reasons:
  - loss of colonial markets after the breakdown of the Empire,
  - contradictory economic courses of Labour (e.g. nationalization) and Tory governments,
  - failure of managements not to modernize production,
  - no investment in infrastructure (roads, railways).

- Socio-economic reasons:
  - Relations between the strong trade unions and managements became worse in the 60s and 70s.
  - Widespread **strikes** became a real problem, resulting in a situation close to an economic breakdown in the winter 1978/79.

- As a consequence of the economic crisis, conservative Margaret Thatcher was elected Prime Minister in 1979.

Thatcherism and its Consequences

- Margaret Thatcher's (Prime Minister 1979–1990) wide-ranging programme of social and economic reform is often referred to as "Thatcherism".

- Privatization, cuts and the concept of self-reliance:
  - privatization of many previously state-controlled industries, such as British Telecom, British Rail or British Airways,
  - tax cuts for entrepreneurs and other top earners to encourage investment,
  - cuts on government's expenses, in particular on welfare programmes,
  - stressing the responsibility of the individual,
  - creating an atmosphere of competition and efficiency,
  - drastically reducing the power of trade unions.

- Positive results:
  - Thatcherism **reversed** the 30-year negative trend in Britain's prosperity.
  - Dramatic reduction of the number of strikes,
  - continuous drop of inflation.

- Criticism:
  - sharp rise in unemployment,
  - loss of the previously strong sense of community.

- For her strict (domestic and international) course Margaret Thatcher was called the "Iron Lady".

- The "New Labour" governments under Tony Blair continued the successful policies of the Conservatives and combined them with many of the EU Social Chapter reforms.

Challenges of the Post-Thatcher Economy

- For 17 years, up to 2008, the UK economy experienced an unprecedented boom.
- The world-wide economic crisis of 2008 hit Britain hard, because
  - it is one of the most globalized countries,
  - it is vulnerably dependent on international markets,
  - the financial sector is at the centre of British economy (10% of the GDP).
- Unemployment
  - Many inner city districts and former industrial areas suffer from severe unemployment.
  - At 20% the unemployment of young people (18–24 years) is up to three times the overall rate.
  - Black unemployment for youngsters rose to more than 40% in 2013.
  - Since 2012 the economy has been on the road to recovery. The overall unemployment rate dropped from 8.3% to 7.1% in 2014.
- Gap between rich and poor has widened.
- Difference between a wealthy South and a rather poor North.

Structural Changes in the Last Decades

- Like other countries of the Western world, Britain has experienced a change from manufacturing to service industries.

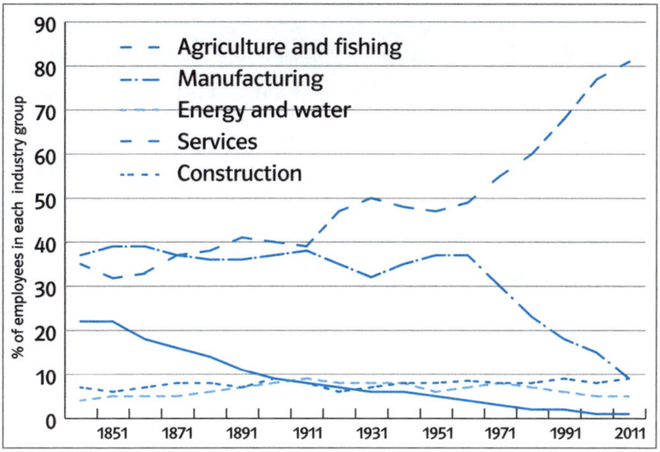

ONS, Census

- Different regional development:
  - decline of the traditional heavy industry (steel, coal) in South Wales, the Midlands and the North,
  - growth of new technology (aerospace, IT, chemical and plastic industries) in Scotland and the South-East.

- After the discovery of oil in the North Sea Britain has become independent with respect to its energy needs. Today the UK is the world's fifth largest oil-producing country.

A Prosperous South and a Poor North

- With respect to unemployment, income, GDP and quality of life, Britain is a geographically, politically, socially and economically divided country.

North		South	
North East	27900	East of London	48100
North West	29900	London	54300
Yorkshire & the Humber	35700	South East	69400
East Midlands	41600	South West	49600
West Midlands	34500		
Wales	34700		
Scotland	39600		

Office for National Statistics
in pound by household 2010

Wealth in different regions

- Industrial decay in the Midlands and the North which went along with a new prosperity in the South widened the long-lasting gap.

- Politically, the South votes Conservative, whereas the North supports Labour.

- Alarming difference in the quality of teaching and students' performance with poorer results in the North.

- Difference in health and mortality rate: People in the North of England are 20% more likely to die before they reach the age of 75 than those in the South.

T. C. Boyle: *The Tortilla Curtain* (Novel, 1995)

- The novel is about problems of illegal immigrants.

- Plot
  - Cándido Rincón (aged 33) and his young pregnant wife América (17) are two homeless illegal Mexican immigrants, living in a provisional shack in Topanga Canyon near Los Angeles.
  - Delaney Mossbacher, who has recently moved into a gated community on top of Topanga, hits and injures Cándido by car.
  - For different reasons, each man prefers not to call the police or an ambulance. Cándido is afraid of being deported and Delaney is afraid of ruining his perfect driving record. Delaney soothes his conscience by giving Cándido "$ 20 blood money".
  - Due to the accident, Cándido is unable to work or to find another job; finally the couple has to look through the garbage cans behind fast food restaurants in order not to starve.
  - A fire accidentally caused by Cándido requires the gated community of Topanga to be evacuated.
  - In the midst of the escalating disasters, Delaney is about to confront the Mexican with a gun, when Cándido's shack is knocked over in a landslide. Cándido and América manage to save themselves, but their daughter Socorro drowns in a river.
  - Although Cándido has been threatened by Delaney, he helps him out of the river. With this surprising twist the novel ends.

- The **American Dream** of the Mexican immigrants turns into a nightmare.

Arthur Miller: *Death of a Salesman* (Drama, 1949)

- Plot
  - Willy Loman, a 63-year-old unsuccessful salesman, is a psychologically unstable character as he tends to imagine events from the past as if they were real. He also talks a lot to himself.
  - He is not only disappointed about his own life, but also about the failure of his two sons Biff and Harold ("Happy").
  - Biff has dropped out of high school. Lacking ambition, he does not know whether he should start a career as a businessman or a farmer.
  - Both Willy's and Biff's plans for a new start are shattered in the course of the play.
  - Additionally, the relation between father and son is full of tension because Biff once witnessed Willy having an affair on one of his sales trips in Boston.
  - Biff tries to reconcile with his father, arguing that Willy should let go his unrealistic high expectations for both of them.
  - At the end of the play the audience gets the impression that Willy kills himself by crashing his car so that Biff can use the life insurance money to start his business.

- The **American Dream** does not work out in the Loman family:
  - Willy works hard until exhaustion but is not successful,
  - Biff already fails at school,
  - Happy is an unimportant assistant,
  - Willy's dead brother became rich by criminal means only.

Arthur Miller: *The Crucible* (Drama, 1953)

- Dramatized and partially fictionalized story of the **Salem witch trials** that took place in Massachusetts during 1692 and 1693.

- Plot
  - When some girls are seen in a harmless love-spell ritual, they start accusing other women of being bewitched.
  - Abigail Williams, the 17-year-old antagonist of the play, once had an affair with John Proctor whom she still loves.
  - Abigail tries to use the town's fear of witches to her advantage. She wants Elizabeth Proctor out of the way so that she and John can marry, as a consequence of which she finally accuses Elizabeth of witchcraft.
  - At court, accusations turn against Proctor himself. In a climate of fear more than a hundred people are arrested.
  - In prison, Proctor asks for his wife Elizabeth's forgiveness. She says he needs to forgive himself. Elizabeth blames herself for the affair, claiming to be a "cold wife".
  - For the sake of his children's reputation, Proctor refuses to sign a written confession that he is the devil's man. He stays true to himself and accepts death. The curtain falls just before Proctor is hanged.

- Miller's intention was to criticize the American political climate in the 1950s:
  - He wrote the play as an allegory of **McCarthyism**, when the US government blacklisted accused communists.
  - Miller himself was questioned by the House of Representatives' Committee on Un-American Activities in 1956.

- The drama shows how wrong personal choices lead to a challenge to society.

Jeannette Walls: *Half Broke Horses* (Novel, 2009)

- The novel deals with the personal challenges and choices of the protagonist Lily Casey, the author's grandmother.

- In her childhood, she successfully meets the challenges of the rough land on the ranch with its poor soil, the lack of water, natural disasters (thunderstorms, floods) and serious diseases.

- Lily learns to **rely on herself** when she
  - opts for a good education at a Catholic school in Santa Fe,
  - goes to Chicago on her own,
  - takes various teaching jobs in the middle of nowhere.

- Economic challenges:
  - At the time of the Great Depression (1929–1934) Lily and her husband fail to pay back their loans for their garage and go bankrupt.
  - Despite managing two ranches (1934–1939), they have very little money. Lily's jobs such as teaching, cleaning, driving a school bus and running a taxi service help them to survive.

- Confronted with death (fatal accident of her friend Minnie, suicide of her sister Helen, her parents' death), Lily often makes a conscious decision to move on, which shows her typically pragmatic, future-oriented, optimistic way of thinking.

- Problems with husband and children:
  - When Lily finds out that her first husband already has a family, she annuls the marriage.
  - She fails in making her children appreciate the value of education as Rosemary and Little Jim hate boarding school.
  - Against her will, she finally has to accept her daughter Rosemary's choice of Rex as her husband.

Crash (Film, 2004)

- The episodic film *Crash* by Paul Haggis is about 36 hours in the lives of 14 characters who accidentally bump into each other in multi-ethnic Los Angeles.

- Portrayal of contemporary challenges to American society:
  - tensions within multicultural society,
  - deeply rooted **racism,**
  - violence and crime.

- **Individual challenges and choices:**
  - White Officer John Ryan's racist attitude is questioned when he has to rescue Christine out of the burning car.
  - Officer Hansen's outspoken non-racist behaviour is challenged by the African American hitch-hiker Peter, who he finally kills in an act of self-defence.
  - Jean Cabot's hidden bias against minorities is revealed. Finally she has to recognize that her Hispanic housekeeper Maria is her best friend.
  - Cameron and Christine Thayer are discriminated because of their skin colour, although they belong to the upper class. Cameron risks his life in being provocative to the police.
  - Detective Graham Waters fails in finding and taking care of his brother.
  - The stereotypical African American car thief Anthony tries to make money out of everything, but refrains from selling the illegal refugees in his stolen car. Instead, he sets them free.
  - Farhad, an Iranian store-owner, is faced with Islamophobia after 9/11, as a consequence of which his shop is demolished. In his frustration, he tries to kill Daniel, the Hispanic locksmith.

- The **viewers'** own preconceptions and prejudices are challenged when characters turn out to be different to prior expectations.

Outsourced (Film, 2006)

- The American movie is a romantic comedy which deals with economic challenges and cultural differences in a globalized world.

- Todd Anderson is in charge of a call centre of an American company in Seattle, which is outsourced to India to reduce costs.

- His tasks are to
  - train his own Indian successor Puro,
  - teach the Indians to sound American,
  - reduce the average call of the members of staff from 12 to 6 minutes.

- Anderson fails to achieve his goals because he
  - hates being in India,
  - is totally ignorant of the Indian culture.

- Only when he falls in love with Asha, he is ready to accept India and its culture. As a consequence he changes from a disillusioned grumbling man to an open-minded cosmopolitan.

- Ironically, the call centre is again shifted to China due to even cheaper labour costs over there. That means the end of Anderson's relation with Asha.

Aldous Huxley: *Brave New World* (Novel, 1932)

- Having witnessed revolutionary changes in psychology (Freud) and the application of mass production in industry, Huxley anticipated developments in reproductive technology, sleep-learning and classical conditioning.

- Unlike the most popular optimist utopian novels of the time, Huxley sought to provide a frightening vision of the future.

- The **dystopian** World State is built upon the principles of **Henry Ford's** assembly line:
  - People are artificially generated in a mass production process in a laboratory.
  - Ford himself is revered as the creator of the society, e.g. by celebrations of "Ford Day" or oaths by his name ("By Ford!"). Christian crosses are cut off for the worship of the "T".
  - The World State calendar starts with "AF" ("Anno Ford"), the year in which Ford's first Model T rolled off the assembly line.

- The state's motto "Community, Identity, Stability" is guaranteed by
  - a strictly controlled, stratified society in which everyone lives according his/her genetically engineered abilities,
  - psychological manipulation by the hypnopaedic process, which provides everyone with subconscious messages appropriate to their caste,
  - everybody's happiness,
  - sexual promiscuity,
  - the ready availability and consumption of the drug soma.

- Nonconformists (e.g. John and his mother) live in savage reservations. At the end the protagonist Bernard Marx is exiled.

George Orwell: *Nineteen Eighty-Four* (Novel, 1949)

- The dystopian novel is modelled on Stalin's totalitarian dictatorship in the Soviet Union.

- The title is believed to be a permutation of 1948, the year of composition.

- After atomic wars there are only three superstates left, which are permanently at war with each other.

- The tyranny of the privileged inner party is ensured by propaganda and total surveillance:
  - "**Big Brother** is watching you",
  - posters of the Party leader dominate the city,
  - telescreen monitors control the private and public lives of the populace,
  - thought control,
  - manipulating history by adapting it to the present conditions.

- The government is divided into four departments. Their Newspeak terms satirically reveal their true nature:
  - the Ministry of Love (Miniluv) is responsible for brainwashing,
  - the Ministry of Plenty (Miniplenty) administers shortage and rationing,
  - the Ministry of Peace (Minipax) oversees the perpetual war,
  - the Ministry of Truth (Minitrue) controls propaganda.

- Plot:
  - The outer party member Winston Smith falls in love with Julia.
  - Their secret rebellion is betrayed, so that he is sent to Room 101, where every prisoner is confronted with his worst fear and broken by torture.

Ray Bradbury: *Fahrenheit 451* (Novel, 1953)

- The dystopian novel presents a future American society in which books are forbidden.

- The title refers to the temperature at which specialized firemen burn all books. Fahrenheit 451 equals 242 degrees Celsius.

- Plot
  - Guy Montag, a fireman hired to burn the property of anyone who read books, begins to question the system.
  - He steals a Bible from a home he has to put on fire and starts reading literature.
  - His uninspired wife Mildred and her friends do not care about politics or being manipulated by "parlor walls", large television screens in their living-rooms.
  - In the end, Montag's obsession for books is uncovered; after he has to burn down his own house, he flees to a group of book-lovers in the countryside.
  - There he witnesses the annihilation of the city by a nuclear attack. Together with the other rebels, he starts rebuilding society.

- Themes
  - Bradbury stated that he was deeply concerned about US censorship and the threat of banishing books in the **McCarthy era** in the early 1950s. Early in his lifetime he had seen the burning of literature in Nazi Germany.
  - Loss of importance of books in the time of other mass media (radio, TV).
  - Dangers of an illiterate society unaware of being manipulated by mass media (cf. Montag's wife).
  - Resistance against forced conformity.

Suzanne Collins: *The Hunger Games* (Trilogy, 2008–2010)

- The *Hunger Games* trilogy takes place in an unspecified future time in a dystopian post-apocalyptic nation of Panem, in the ruins of North America. The country consists of
  - the wealthy and technologically advanced Capitol,
  - suppressed twelve (formerly thirteen) districts in varying states of poverty.

- *The Hunger Games* (2008)
  - One boy and one girl from each of the twelve districts are selected by lottery to participate in the annual "Hunger Games", televised death games in which only one survives.
  - The protagonist Katniss Everdeen is a 16-year-old girl from District 12 who survives the games along with Peeta Mellark when they both defy the Capitol by threatening to commit suicide.

- *Catching Fire* (2009)
  - Katniss's resistance has sparked off rebellion in the districts. The mockingjay pin she wears becomes its symbol.
  - In the 75th edition of the *Hunger Games*, known as the "Quarter Quell", she is forced to fight again alongside Peeta.
  - Unintentionally, she becomes an integral part of the rebellion when she destroys the arena and escapes the Games.
  - Katniss's district 12 is destroyed.

- *Mockingjay* (2010)
  - Concentrates on the rebellion of the districts.
  - Led by district 13, the rebels overthrow the Capitol's regime.

Common Features of Dystopias

- Dystopias (i.e. negative utopian visions) unfold future worlds often characterized by totalitarian governments and strictly hierarchical social stratification in an urban setting hostile to nature.

- Political layout:
  - concentration of political power in one or more superstates on the ruins of present-day nations,
  - setup of a **totalitarian dictatorship**, able to control most aspects of politics, economy and society,
  - dystopian government establishments often cause protagonists or groups to resist against the system.

- Society:
  - stark contrasts between the privileges of the ruling class and the dreary existence of the working classes,
  - repressing intellectuals with particular force,
  - mostly hostile to the concept of "family", some have even eradicated it altogether.

- Violence is prevalent in form of
  - radical governmental politics,
  - war and rebellion.

- Nature
  - Fictional dystopias are commonly urban; in contrast, nature functions as a retreat for nonconformists or rebels.
  - Science and technology are used to control nature, including human natural instincts.
  - Dystopian films (e.g. *Avatar*) often portray an environmentally polluted and destroyed nature.

The Globe – Shakespeare's Theatre

- Since 1599 Shakespeare and his company (**The Lord Chamberlain's Men**) had a theatre of their own on the right side of the River Thames: the Globe.

- Everything we know about Shakespearean theatres is from the copy of a sketch by a Dutch traveller (the original is lost).

Drawing of "The Swan", another playhouse at that time (ca. 1596)

- Structure and layout
  - The Globe was a round or octagonal building with an apron stage in the middle of the open-air courtyard and three rows of roofed galleries for the spectators of higher ranks.
  - Lower-class people, the so-called groundlings, stood around the stage.
  - The rear part of the stage was covered by a roof. Above there was a kind of gallery which might have been used for scenes that require an upper level.

- Stage productions
  - As there was no artificial light, performances took place in the afternoon.
  - There was no scenery.
  - Female parts were played by men.

The Elizabethan World Picture

- The Elizabethan world was in a **state of flux**; people were confused and frightened as traditional beliefs were challenged by new scientific discoveries and the exploration of new parts of the world.

- Central ideas of the epoch were the belief in a universal order, the Great Chain of Being, the four elements, the signs of the zodiac and the determination by fate.

- World of **correspondences** (Great Chain of Being)
  - Cosmic and human conditions are linked together.
  - The relation of the monarch and his subjects equals the relation of God and its creation.
  - Social disruption (e.g. Macbeth's upheaval in Shakespeare's tragedy) corresponds to natural disorder (e.g. the thunder-storm in *Macbeth*).

- The Four Elements and the Four Humours
  - There was a strong belief that everything that existed was made from a combination of the four elements: Fire, Air, Water and Earth.
  - The four elements had their counterparts in the four humours of the human body: blood, phlegm, black bile (melancholy) and yellow bile (choler). If any of these humours predominated in the body, they determined the mood of the person.

- The Wheel of Fortune
  - Fate (or Fortune) was believed to be the main controlling force in life.
  - Just as part of a wheel moves from a low to a high position or from high to low, so does a man's life.
  - Stars predetermined people's fate.

Romeo and Juliet (Tragedy, 1597)

- Plot
  - The play is set in Verona, where the noble families of the Montagues and Capulets are sworn enemies.
  - Nevertheless, Romeo, Montague's son, falls in love with Juliet Capulet. In the so-called "balcony scene" they confess their love to each other.
  - Romeo is exiled from Verona after he has slain Tybalt, Juliet's cousin.
  - Meanwhile Juliet is pressurized into marrying Count Paris.
  - Juliet visits Friar Lawrence for help, and he offers her a potion that will put her into a deathlike sleep for "two and forty hours."
  - The Friar promises to send a messenger to inform Romeo of the plan, so that he can rejoin her when she awakens, but the messenger fails to reach him.
  - Believing Juliet to be dead, Romeo drinks the shortly before acquired poison while sitting next to Juliet in the Capulet's crypt.
  - Juliet then awakens and, finding Romeo dead, stabs herself with his dagger.
  - The families are reconciled by their children's deaths and agree to end their violent feud.

- Themes/motifs:
  - (doomed) love,
  - fate and chance,
  - time (duality of density and haste),
  - duality of light (love) and dark (death).

Baz Luhrmann: *Romeo + Juliet* (Film, 1996)

- The film is an abridged modernization of Shakespeare's play.
- While it retains the original Shakespearean dialogue, a lot of changes have been made.
- Setting and Costumes
  - Instead of Verona, Italy, the tragedy is set in the fictional seaside metropolis "Verona Beach", resembling modern Miami.
  - The Montague boys parade around in Hawaiian shirts, while the Capulet boys favour leather and metal-heeled boots.
  - Swords are replaced with guns (with brand names such as "Dagger" and "Sword").
- Characters
  - Some characters' names have been adapted to modern America (e.g. Ted Montague, Father Lawrence).
  - The Montagues and the Capulets are represented as warring mafia empires (with legal business fronts).
- Plot
  - At the end of the so-called "balcony scene" Romeo and Juliet fall into the mansion's pool.
  - Juliet awakens just as Romeo takes the poison; the two thus see each other before he dies.
  - After Romeo dies, Juliet picks up his gun and shoots herself in the head, dying instantly.
- Imagery
  - Water plays an important role, symbolizing the purity of Romeo's and Juliet's love. Both characters are often shown under water.

Othello (Tragedy, 1603/04)

- Plot
  - Othello, a black general in the Venetian army, has secretly married Desdemona.
  - Othello's jealous captain Iago hates **the Moor** for promoting a younger man named Michael Cassio above him. He is also angry because he believes that Othello might have slept with his wife Emilia.
  - In his intrigue Iago makes use of Othello's hot temper. He persuades Othello to be suspicious of Cassio and Desdemona.
  - When Othello accidentally drops a handkerchief that was his first gift to his wife, Iago plants it among Cassio's possessions.
  - On finding it, Othello is manipulated and made to believe that Cassio has an affair with Desdemona. Enraged and hurt, Othello resolves to kill his wife and asks Iago to kill Cassio.
  - In the night Othello smothers Desdemona in their own bed.
  - When Othello discovers that he has been deceived and killed his innocent wife, he stabs himself.

- Themes:
  - racism,
  - love and jealousy,
  - betrayal,
  - revenge,
  - repentance.

The Merchant of Venice (Comedy, 1596–98)

- Plot
  - Bassanio, a young Venetian nobleman, is desperate for money to court the rich heiress Portia of Belmont.
  - His friend Antonio, a Merchant of Venice, who is outspokenly anti-Semitic and has mistreated the **Jewish moneylender Shylock** several times, acts as loan-guarantor.
  - Shylock lends the money under the condition that he is allowed to take one pound of Antonio's flesh, if the merchant should be unable to pay back the loan.
  - Bassanio marries Portia.
  - Antonio's ships are reported lost at sea so the merchant cannot repay the bond.
  - Shylock has become more determined to take revenge from Christians because his daughter Jessica eloped with a Christian.
  - The climax of the play takes place in the court of the Duke of Venice. Shylock refuses Bassanio's offer of 6,000 ducats. He is about to take his pound of flesh from Antonio with a knife.
  - Portia, disguised as a male lawyer, successfully convinces the court that Shylock, as a Jew and therefore an "alien", having attempted to take the life of a citizen, has forfeited his property.
  - The Duke pardons Shylock's life, but he has to convert to Christianity.

- **Anti-Semitism**
  - Although Shakespeare classified the play as a comedy, modern audiences rather understand Shylock's fate and the displayed anti-Semitic attitudes as tragic.
  - English society in the Elizabethan era has been described as "judeophobic". English Jews had been expelled under Edward I.
  - On the Elizabethan stage, Jews were often presented as caricatures, with hooked noses and bright red wigs.

A Midsummer Night's Dream (Comedy, 1595/96)

- The play consists of four interconnected plots, linked by a celebration of the wedding of Duke Theseus of Athens and the Amazon queen, Hippolyta.

- The Workmen
  - The ridiculous acting troupe prepares for a play to be presented at the wedding.
  - Their final performance is so poor that their tragic play is taken for a comedy.

- Hermia and Lysander
  - have escaped to a forest in hopes of eloping.
  - However, Lysander is taken for his rival Demetrius and given a love potion so that he falls in love with Helena who herself fancies Demetrius.
  - The four quarrel with each other, until Lysander finally turns back to Hermia and Demetrius starts loving Helena.

- Oberon and Titania
  - Oberon, the king of fairies, wants to punish his wife Titania for her disobedience. He squeezes a magical juice onto her eyelids while she is sleeping so that Titania will fall in love with the first creature she sees upon waking.
  - Titania then has a crush on Bottom, a bewitched member of the workmen's acting troupe, who wears a donkey's head.
  - Finally, Oberon releases Titania and arranges everything so that Hermia, Lysander, Demetrius and Helena will believe that they have been dreaming when they awaken.

- Puck's final address to the audience suggests that the enacted "visions" might be dreams.

The Interest of Young Audiences in Shakespeare

- The relevance of Shakespeare for young people today can be concluded from his iconic status as a writer, the artistry of his works, his topics and his unique illumination of human nature.

- **"The Bard's"** worldwide reputation
  - Shakespeare is a central part of British and European cultural heritage.
  - His plays are still the most frequently staged ones.
  - *Romeo and Juliet*, *Hamlet* and *Macbeth* rank in the German top ten.
  - There are many modern film adaptions for a mass audience, e.g. Baz Luhrmann's version *of Romeo + Juliet* (1996).

- Artistic value:
  - construction of complex plots, e.g. *A Midsummer Night's Dream* or *Hamlet* with their plays within the play,
  - poetic language in sonnets and plays.
  - Some idioms and metaphors have become part of ordinary language (e.g. "To be, or not be, that is the question", *Hamlet* III,1,55).

- **Timeless topics:**
  - absoluteness of love,
  - hatred, jealousy, revenge and murder as part of the human psyche,
  - restoration of a well-ordered world despite the constant threat of the powers of evil.

Joseph Conrad: *An Outpost of Progress* (Short Story, 1896)

- Kayerts and Carlier, two white colonizers in Belgian Congo, are absolutely incompetent in running an outstation in the middle of nowhere.
- Their inability is expressed by
  - their funny outer appearance (Kayerts is short and fat, his assistant Carlier is tall and thin),
  - their childish behaviour (i.e. they walk hand in hand),
  - the fact that they do not work.
- When Makola, the African station hand, trades the native workers for ivory, the local tribe stops its support for the outstation so that the colonizers have no food anymore.
- In a fight over the remaining sugar Kayerts accidentally kills his companion, as a consequence of which he commits suicide.
- Use of **irony** in order to ridicule colonial rule:
  - The colonizers bring slavery, destruction and death instead of progress (cf. the title of the story).
  - Kayerts hangs himself from the cross which expresses a denial of Christianity.
  - In an instance of disrespectfulness, the corpse points a swollen tongue to the arriving Managing Director.
- Like many white colonial writers, Joseph Conrad wanted to criticize imperialism.

Rabbit-Proof Fence (Film, 2002)

- The Australian film deals with the "**Stolen Generations**", a governmental policy under which Aboriginal children were taken from their families to be brought up in Christian missionary schools.

- It is loosely based on the **true story** of Molly Pilkington Garimara, who ran away from the Moore River Native Settlement, north of Perth, to return to her Aboriginal family in 1931.

- The film follows three Aboriginal girls as they walk for nine weeks along 1,500 miles of the Australian rabbit-proof fence – designed to keep animals away from agricultural land – to finally arrive at their community at Jigalong.
  - At the beginning, 14-year-old Molly, her 8-year-old sister Daisy and their 10-year-old cousin Gracie are taken from their mothers against their will.
  - At the re-education camp the girls are treated badly, resulting in their decision to escape.
  - Following the rabbit-proof fence is their only chance to find their way back.
  - They are pursued by white law enforcement authorities and an Aboriginal tracker.
  - Gracie is tricked into separating from the two sisters when she gets the deliberately spread, but false information that her mother will wait for her at a train station. There she gets caught by the authorities.
  - With the help of others Molly and Daisy make it to Jigalong. In order to hide together with their mother, they move into the outback.

- Conservative Whites who tend to play down the use of force against Aboriginals criticize the lack of historical accuracy.

Ngugi wa Thiong'o: *A Meeting in the Dark* (Short Story, 1974)

- After decolonization many African authors pointed to the difficult legacy of the British Empire.
- Christian Missionary Schools had helped to develop an educated African elite. On the other hand thay had
  - split African societies into those who followed old traditions and those who adopted values and practices of the colonizers,
  - destroyed traditional beliefs and culture.
- Plot
  - The story is set in Kenya.
  - John, the son of a strict black African Christian clergyman, impregnates Wamuhu, a circumcised girl from the local village tribe.
  - "Caught between the two cultures" (cf. his dream), he feels torn apart.
  - John has to decide between marrying Wamuhu or going to university in Uganda.
  - Finally, he kills his girlfriend to hide his parenthood, mainly out of fear of his father.

Salman Rushdie: *Good Advice Is Rarer than Rubies* (Short Story, 1994)

- Plot
  - Miss Rehana, the story's protagonist, is an independent, self-confident Pakistani woman. In contrast to others, she comes to the British Consulate for her immigration papers barefaced and on her own.
  - The advertisements ("MOVE OVER DARLING", "O.K. GOOD-LIFE") at the front and back of the coach with which she arrives foreshadows her dilemma.
  - She has to decide whether she wants to continue her self-determined life as a nanny in a large Pakistani house or move to England to marry Mustafa Dar, a totally unknown man to whom she has been promised when she was a child.
  - Muhammad Ali, a petty crook selling British passports to turned-down Pakistani women, tries to frighten her with the information that the British staff will ask her questions of very personal nature in order to single out frauds.
  - To his surprise, Miss Rehana later tells him that she has deliberately answered all questions wrong in the interview, so that she is denied the required visa.
  - She happily returns to Lahore.

- Miss Rehana stands for
  - the growing **self-confidence** of the former colonial subjects towards Britain,
  - the trend not to emigrate to Britain in order to seek a better future.

Hanif Kureishi: *My Son the Fanatic* (Short Story, 1994)

- At the centre of the story there is a **father-and-son conflict**, revealing different strategies of dealing with their Pakistani cultural roots.

- Parvez, a middle-aged taxi driver in Bradford, has completely **assimilated** into the British culture which is shown by his
  - eating pork and drinking beer,
  - contact to the prostitute Bettina whom he takes home in his taxi for free ("a ride in exchange for a ride").

- His son, Ali, has been integrated, but he
  - quits his job as an accountant and becomes a community worker for Muslim prisoners,
  - parts from his English girlfriend,
  - gives away all his belongings typical for a British young man.

- While Parvez has abandoned any contact to religion (after a traumatic experience with a mullah in Lahore), Ali has found some orientation in the Muslim mosque; he starts praying.

- An attempt to talk about their different lifestyles and points of view fails. Ali seems to follow radical Muslim fundamentalist ideas when he mentions the jihad and his readiness to die.

- Finally the situation escalates as the drunken Parvez hits his son in despair. In a dramatic turn Ali asks him: "So who's the fanatic now?"

- Kureishi's story shows
  - the difference between first- and second-generation immigrants,
  - the lack of **cultural identity** of these British-born immigrants,
  - the way of second-generation immigrants turning to **fundamentalism** or eventually becoming terrorists.

Qaisra Shahraz: *A Pair of Jeans* (Short Story, 1988, 2004)

- The story deals with the topic of **arranged marriages** and the emancipation of women in Britain's multicultural society.
- Miriam, a Pakistani university student in a Northern British town, lives in two different worlds:
  - Outside her home, she enjoys the freedom of other young British women. There she dresses in a western way, with a tight pair of jeans and a shirt showing her midriff.
  - Inside her (rather liberal) Pakistani home, she has to wear traditional clothes (shalwar, kameez) of a Muslim girl.
- Her marriage with Farook has been arranged by their parents. She is not at all against the tradition of arranged marriages; apart from that she likes her fiancé.
- The story's conflict arises when she comes home from a day out with her English friends. Dressed in a western way, she bumps into her conservative future parents-in-law Ayub and Begum.
- After this experience Ayub and Begum call off the arranged marriage with their son Farook, because they fear that Miriam
  - does not fit in their household,
  - takes drugs or might have had a boyfriend/sex before,
  - might twine their son around her fingers.
- Two different endings
  - In the first ending of 1988 Miriam angrily accepts the cancellation of her wedding and throws away her jeans.
  - In the **second ending** – added in 2004 – Miriam takes her western clothes back on and calls Farook to discuss their future relation.
  - With the second ending Sharaz reflected on the different level of **emancipation** among Pakistani women since 1988.

Bali Rai: *(Un)Arranged Marriage* (Novel, 2001)

- As the title suggests, the young-adult novel deals with the culture practice of arranged marriages in British Indian communities.

- Manjit ("Manny"), a Punjabi teenager living in Leicester, is the protagonist and first-person narrator of the novel. He is often in trouble because he
  - runs away from home,
  - commits little crimes,
  - skives school lessons,
  - has bad marks at school,
  - has fallen in love with Lisa, a white British girl,
  - wants to be a normal English teenager,
  - does not meet his father's expectations of living according to Punjabi traditions.

- Plot
  - At the age of 13, Manjit gets to know that his parents have promised him to an unknown girl from India for his 17th birthday. From the beginning he is against that plan.
  - When the family travels to India, Manjit is culturally shocked and soon feels homesick.
  - He is left alone in India by his parents who secretly fly back to England.
  - With the help of the family's black sheep, his uncle Jag who lives a western lifestyle in India, Manjit gets back home.
  - He pretends to follow his father's plan of the arranged marriage, but in the middle of the wedding party he escapes.

- Throughout the plot people outside Manjit's family encourage him to live his own life, a piece of advice he finally follows.

East is East (Film, 1999)

- The comedy-drama film deals with difficulties of a **mixed-ethnicity** British household headed by a Pakistani father and an English mother.
- It is set in Salford, Greater Manchester, in 1971, which had a small Pakistani community only.
- Jahangir "George" Khan, a stubborn first-generation Pakistani immigrant, has been married to Ella for 25 years, although he has got a second wife in Pakistan.
- Ella has never had the power to stand up to her dominant husband so that all their seven children have had to grow up according to strict Muslim traditions.
- The children themselves who were born and brought up in Britain
  - increasingly see themselves as British,
  - reject Pakistani customs of dress, food, religion and living,
  - want to decide themselves on their marriage partner.
- This antagonism leads to a rise in tensions and conflicts within the family unit during which the family almost breaks apart.
  - The oldest son Nazir flees from an arranged marriage into a homosexual relationship in Paris.
  - Tariq "Tony" rebels against his father when his marriage is arranged.
  - When Ella bravely confronts her husband to listen to their children's own future plans and ideas, George beats her up. As a consequence, the whole family wants him to leave.
  - The ending, however, suggests that the couple goes on as before.

Bend It Like Beckham (Film, 2002)

- The title of the comedy-drama film refers to the football player David Beckham and his skill at scoring from free kicks by "bending" the ball past a wall of defenders.

- The movie is about Jesminder "Jess" Bhamra, the 18-year-old daughter of Punjabi Sikhs in London. She is infatuated with football but her parents have forbidden her to play because she is a girl.

- Her skills draw the attention of Juliette "Jules" Paxton, who plays for the women's team of the fictional Hounslow Harriers. Jules and Jess become best friends, but both are attracted to their trainer Joe which threatens their relationship.

- In order to play with the team, Jess
  - pretends to have a job,
  - makes her sister cover up her playing in an important match in Germany.

- The decisive match
  - While Jess's family is distracted by the elaborate preparations for her sister Pinky's upcoming wedding, Jess continues to play and the Hounslow Harriers make their way towards the top of the league.
  - On the wedding day Jess's father at last breaks with his obstructive attitude and allows her to play in the final match.
  - Jess and Jules get a scholarship from an American college and go to the USA.

- The *Times of India* noted the film's **social context**, arguing that it "is really about the bending of rules, social paradigms and lives."

Poverty as a Global Challenge

- Facts
  - In 2015 about 702.1 million people lived in extreme poverty.
  - Of these, about 347.1 million people lived in Sub-Saharan Africa (35.2% of the population) and 231.3 million lived in South Asia (13.5% of the population).
  - UNICEF estimates half the world's children live in poverty.
  - According to the United Nations, about 21,000 people die every day of hunger or hunger-related causes.

- Causes of poverty:
  - (post-)colonial consequences such as concentration of wealth in industrialized countries in the Northern hemisphere,
  - continuation of exploitation patterns,
  - brain drain in third world countries,
  - lack of education,
  - overpopulation,
  - climatic reasons.

- Consequences:
  - "poverty cycle": poor people are likely to suffer from poor health, homelessness, lack of security, exclusion, discrimination and lower life expectancy,
  - migration.

- Poverty reduction
  - Between 1990 and 2015, the percentage of the world's population living in extreme poverty fell from 37.1% to 9.6%.
  - Nevertheless, given the current economic model built on GDP, it would take 100 years to bring the world's poorest up to the standard poverty line of $ 1.25 a day.

Migration

- Three major trends of current global migration can be observed.

- Attraction of the USA:
  - emigration from Asian countries like India, the Philippines and China,
  - Central American flows to the US.

- High pressure on Europe:
  - asylum-seekers from the Middle-East,
  - African migration out of economic and political reasons.

- Destination: Australia
  - South African emigration,
  - dropouts from the UK.

- Reasons for migration:
  - war or civil war (e.g. Syria),
  - political or religious persecution,
  - lack of perspective in people's home country,
  - unequal distribution of wealth (North-South-divide).

Environmental Challenges

- Depletion of the ozone layer:
  - Dangerous holes in ozone layer over the Poles are believed to be caused by man-made pollutants.
  - Serious consequences of this process are the disruption of life cycles of plants and the food chain as well as human skin cancer.

- Consequences of **global warming** (caused by large-scale CO_2 emission and other greenhouse gases):
  - melting of artic ice causing sea levels to rise,
  - regional climate changes affecting crop yields and water supplies,
  - diseases such as malaria carried by mosquitos will spread further,
  - natural disasters are expected to be more frequent,
  - some species will become extinct.

- Acid rain
  - contaminates lakes and rivers,
  - damages vegetation (i.e. reduces crown density of trees).

- Environmental pollution
  - problem of waste disposal,
  - use of plastics.

- Approximately 40% of the world's agricultural land is seriously degraded. In Africa, if current trends of soil degradation continue, the continent might be able to feed just 25% of its population by 2025.

- All these processes are very complex, possibly irreversible and require an international solution.

Americanization: Consequences of a Global Culture

- American culture has spread worldwide due to the following facts:
  - Hollywood movies with their unobtrusive portrayal of US values and fashion are global sensations; American television series are points of reference around the globe,
  - popularity of American music,
  - brands like Coke, McDonalds or Nike are available and considered trendy in most countries,
  - the political importance and economic power of the USA.
- Pros
  - American values such as freedom and democracy often go along with or follow cultural trends,
  - availability of standardized quality products.
- Cons
  - destruction of local taste and traditions,
  - simple copying discourages building up own identities.

English as a World Language

- Today up to 1.4 billion people around the world speak English. For more than 800 million it is a lingua franca.

- The growth of English has nothing to do with the structure of the language or any inherent qualities, but rather with politics.

- Legacy of the **British Empire**
  - English Puritans brought their language to the American colonies.
  - In the process of designing a "United" States, the USA's founders knew the importance of language for national identity.
  - In most parts of the second British Empire, English was the language of business and administration.
  - For a long time, access to English meant access to education, e.g. in the mission schools in Africa or the first universities in India.
  - Although many former colonies became officially multilingual when they gained independence, the English language continued to serve as a common basis for communication.
  - English is now the dominant or official language in 75 territories.

- The rise of the USA
  - With the development of the USA to a world power in the 20th century English was guaranteed its dominant role as the most widely spoken language.
  - America's cultural appeal, its economic and political power has made English the (almost) exclusive language in international business and science.
  - For decades, the USA has been the most innovative technological nation, so English is the language of the technological revolution and the Internet.

Genetic Engineering

- Food engineering
  - **Supporters** of genetically modified crops tend to play down the possible dangerous consequences.
  - They argue with the worldwide growing population and the necessity to rationalize and intensify crop growing, making it independent from plights and diseases.
  - In 2010, crops modified by molecular methods were grown in 29 countries on more than 360 million acres.
  - **Critics** put forward that we put ourselves into the hands of a "food mafia", i.e. international companies who can afford to invest in developing genetically modified food and finally dictate what to eat.
  - They fear that the variety of crops is replaced by one standardized product.
  - They are worried that genetically modified crops cannot be stopped from spreading to areas of conventional agriculture.
  - Last but not least, they are afraid that the genetic manipulation might negatively affect all living beings in the end.

- Should it be allowed to create the perfect human being when it suits us best? Ethically controversially discussed are the following scientific practices:
  - **Cloning** (cf. the sheep "Dolly", 1997): Reproductive cloning of human beings is possible but worldwide prohibited.
  - **Stem cell research** which requires destroying in-vitro fertilized human embryos.
  - **Prenatal diagnostics** which help to discover the sex and serious handicaps of the foetus. However, critics fear the spread of eugenic thinking, i.e. handicapped children might be aborted more easily.
  - **"Social freezing"**: egg freezing for women in career or without a present partner for later use.

Big Data

- Companies like Google collect masses of data in order to create personal profiles by
  - analyzing Internet searches,
  - tracking smart phones.

- Google dreams of selling these profiles (so-called "Big Data") one day, as a result of which companies would be able to **personalize** advertisements, e.g. by combining GPS-position with weather dates and general preferences.

- Most people do not worry about their data when subscribing to commercial companies (e.g. Payback) or social networks such as Facebook, arguing that they have got nothing to hide.

- Others fear
  - the loss of one's private sphere,
  - the beginning of total surveillance, ending up in an Orwellian state of control and manipulation,
  - the misuse of the collected data, e.g. by the NSA or other intelligence agencies.

Social Media

- Social networks like Facebook connect people via the Internet.

- Facebook
  - has more than 600 million users worldwide.
  - In a single day, about a billion new pieces of content are posted on this platform.
  - It also owns the photo/video platform Instagram and the messenger WhatsApp.
  - Altogether, it is the connective tissue for nearly one tenth of the planet.

- Fans of Facebook
  - appreciate the fact that it is free,
  - argue that it is the best way to stay in touch with friends,
  - emphasize the role of social media in organizing people.

- Critics
  - are annoyed about advertisements,
  - are worried about peer pressure to be online,
  - fear that terrorists might plan their actions via these networks,
  - are worried about the importance of virtual "friends",
  - are shocked by the dramatic change of the notion of privacy,
  - are dissatisfied with the company's data protection policies.

- Twitter (with 302 million active accounts) is a social network for short messages (tweets), often used by celebrities, politicians or companies to spread some news. Barack Obama, for example, has 53 million followers.

- Internet-based dating services are said to be involved in initiating one in three relationships today.

Power of Media Corporations

- Globally operating media corporations such as Comcast, Google, Disney, Viacom etc have bigger budgets than some nation states. As agents and moderators of globalization they have enormous economic and opinion-shaping power.
- **Rupert Murdoch**, an Australian-born American media mogul, owns about two per cent of all media worldwide. Among these are
  - the Australian *Sunday Times*, a successful tabloid,
  - the *Australian*, the first nationwide newspaper on that continent,
  - the British quality paper *The Times*,
  - the British most influential tabloid *The Sun*,
  - the British Sky Channel,
  - the former Hollywood Studio 20th Century Fox,
  - the American TV network "Fox",
  - the Asian "STAR TV" channel with 100 million spectators daily,
  - 175 newspapers all over the globe.
- He is criticized for a biased conservative coverage, thus manipulating people's opinions:
  - *The Sun* has an outstanding record for being Eurosceptic and anti-German.
  - "Fox" supports Republican policies. Since 2009 the network tries to show the Obama administration in a bad light.
  - Murdoch publicly admitted that he actively tried to shape public opinion in favour of Bush's Iraq War.

Cartoons

- The analysis of a cartoon requires you to give a detailed description, to reveal the artist's message and to provide background information.

- A description includes
  - a reference to relevant publication details (e.g. the paper's political inclination or its target group),
  - a detailed description of main elements of the sketch (use the present progressive!),
  - mentioning all textual elements.

- Be as explicit as you can with respect to where you can find which detail.

- Revealing the artist's **message** means
  - explicitly stating the artist's aims with the cartoon,
  - working out his devices, e.g. making fun of someone by ...

- Providing **background information** aims at
  - explaining the artist's point of view on the ground of the political, economic or social circumstances,
  - evaluating the artist's claims.

Graphs and Charts

- Graphs and charts visualize the statistic relationship between at least two different variables.

- Three different diagrams are to be distinguished:
  - line graphs, e.g. for showing a development over a period of time,
  - bar charts, for a comparison of two or more elements,
  - pie charts, often used for proportional distribution.

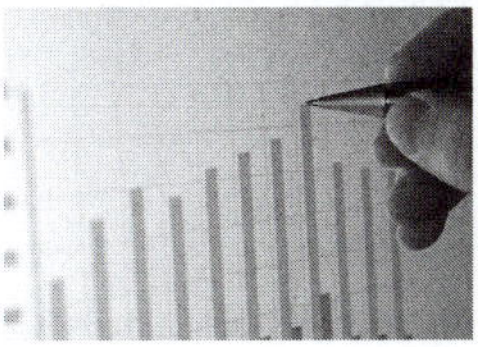
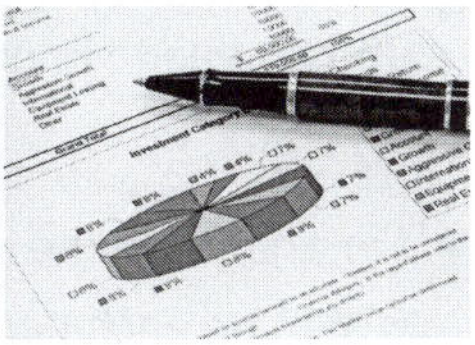

- Crucial is the exact description of what is shown, i.e.
  - a moment or period in time,
  - the character of the presented figures (index, relative or absolute numbers).

- Not all numbers are relevant for interpretation! Watch out for
  - general trends,
  - turning-points,
  - maxima/minima,
  - most striking/surprising figures.

- After a detailed description you need to explain the data on the basis of your background knowledge and comment on them.

Non-fictional Texts

- Non-fiction texts such as journalistic texts or political speeches do not only give information, but use different strategies to
  - make the reader/listener think in a particular direction,
  - convince the recipient of the author's or speaker's point of view,
  - appeal emotionally.

- The analysis of such texts requires a close look at their structure and language in order to uncover the strategies mentioned above.

- For analyzing the **structure**
  - sum up each paragraph by an appropriate headline,
  - note down which function each paragraph has for the text as a whole (e.g. introduction, example, central argument, outlook etc).

- With respect to **language**, look for
  - the register of the text, i.e. the stylistic level (colloquial, formal, use of a certain jargon etc),
  - the tone of the text, e.g. serious, ironic, bitter etc,
  - rhetorical questions,
  - imagery (metaphors and similes),
  - references to history, literature, religion etc,
  - quotations,
  - figures and statistics,
  - word plays.

- You should work out the effects of these stylistic devices, which often lend an air of authority to the views expressed.

Setting

- The setting informs about the **time** and **place** of the plot.

- Depending on the literary genre, the time and place are provided by different means:
  - In a narrative, the author usually gives the reader all information he wants him or her to know; sometimes the reader has to work it out by himself.
  - In traditional performances the setting can be deducted from the scenery, the props and the costumes on the stage.
  - In Shakespeare's time the actors themselves had to inform the audiences, as there was no scenery (e.g. the Chorus in the Prologue of *Romeo and Juliet*: "Two houses both alike in dignity / In fair Verona, where we lay our scene").

- Apart from that, the opening passages of a drama or narrative text have the following functions:
  - introducing one or more characters,
  - setting the atmosphere,
  - foreshadowing forthcoming events (cf. Doris Lessing, "The Second Hut", in: D. L., *Collected African Stories*, vol. 1, London: Michael Joseph, 1973, p. 65: "Before that season and his wife's illness, he had thought things could get no worse"),
  - introducing central themes and motifs,
  - exposing the conflict of the literary work.

Structure of a Classical Drama

- Classical dramas follow the Aristotelian tradition of a **five-act scheme.**

- Exposition (first act)
  - provides the setting,
  - introduces the main characters,
  - prepares for an arising conflict.

- Rising Action (second act)
  - intensification of the conflict.

- Climax and turning point (third act)
  - highest dramatic tension,
  - decisive turning-point for a final happy ending or catastrophe.

- Falling action (fourth act)
  - postpones the ending,
  - often contains some comic relief before the disaster.

- Solution (fifth act)
  - unravelling of all subplots for the final outcome of the conflict,
  - comedy: marriage or at least finding of the lovers,
  - tragedy: downfall (often death) of the protagonist.

- Modern drama has abandoned this form, replacing the five-act scheme with a more flexible structure (e.g. one or two-act plays) and experimenting with non-sequential plots.

Ending

- Endings can be divided into four categories: happy endings, surprise endings, denouements and open endings.

- Happy ending:
  - usually fulfilment of a love relation,
  - to be found in comedies and romantic narratives.

- Surprise ending:
  - sudden twist contrary to the reader's expectation,
  - sometimes foreshadowed in the text but only to be found on close analysis,
  - common in short stories.

- Denouement:
  - resolution of a conflict,
  - often a final decision between two possible alternatives,
  - very often used in short stories and dramas.

- Open ending:
  - The narrative's conflict remains unsolved.
  - It is up to the reader's imagination to figure out how the characters or the action might develop.

Characterization

- You should distinguish between flat and round characters as well as explicit and implicit characterization.

- A **round character** is complex:
  - It has several often quite different character traits,
  - develops in the course of the plot.

- A **flat character** has got no psychological depth:
  - It has no individual identity,
  - does not change,
  - is of minor importance to the plot.

- **Explicit characterization**
  - Detailed description of a person's outward appearance and character.

- **Implicit characterization** is the indirect revelation of a personality by a character's
  - actions,
  - thoughts,
  - language.

Stylistic Devices

- Stylistic devices call for a functional interpretation, i.e. it is your task to uncover their effect and the author's intention.
- Rhetorical questions
  - do not give the reader a chance of answering,
  - manipulate the reader in thinking in a particular way.
- Imagery
  - Metaphors (e.g. "cold heart") and similes (i.e. comparisons with "like" or "as") evoke associations which open new horizons of interpretation.
  - Symbols illustrate abstract concepts (e.g. the coyotes in T. C. Boyle's novel *The Tortilla Curtain* allude to illegal immigration).
- Anaphora
  - The repetitive parallel structure of sentences makes the content of a text more memorable (e.g. "When shall we three meet again / In thunder, lightning, or in rain? / When the hurly-burly's done, / When the battle's lost and won", Shakespeare, *Macbeth* I,1,1–4).
  - An idea can be taken up again and elaborated on.
- Antithesis
  - The juxtaposition of two opposing words, abstract ideas (e.g. "Come, night, come, Romeo, come, thou day in night", Shakespeare, *Romeo and Juliet* III,2,17) or phrases highlights the difference between the two.
- Irony
  - usually has a comic effect,
  - creates a distance,
  - can be tragic (irony of fate).

Narrative Perspective

- Different narrative perspectives allow authors to provide the readers with different levels of insight.

- **Omniscient** narrator
  - towers above all characters,
  - knows all characters' actions, thoughts and feelings,
  - is highly reliable.

- **Third-person** narrator
  - can vary between an almost omniscient and a rather restricted point of view of a single character,
  - is often only an observer.

- **First-person** narrator
  - often is the protagonist of the story,
  - has got a limited point of view,
  - might be wrong in his thoughts and assumptions about others,
  - is unreliable as he might want to hide something or to mislead the reader.

- Modern and postmodern authors often introduce various narrators who tell the main story from different points of view. Their different perceptions add up in the reader's mind.

Letter to the Editor

- A letter to the editor is a comment on a particular article in a newspaper or journal.

- As it is a **formal letter**, it must include
  - your address (in the top right-hand corner),
  - a date (below your address),
  - the receiver's address (in the top left-hand corner),
  - a reference line (i.e. the article you are commenting on).

- Start off your text with
  - addressing the editor by his/her name or "Dear Sir or Madam",
  - referring to the title and content of the newspaper article and your intention.

- In discussing the author's arguments, do not go through all given points but choose the ones which are most important to you or which you find most controversial.

- End your letter with polite formula such as
  - "Yours (sincerely/faithfully)" or
  - "With kind regards".

- Language
  - Be aware of an appropriate style,
  - do not use colloquial or informal expressions,
  - do not use contracted forms such as "can't" or "don't".

Interior Monologue

- An interior monologue offers a deep-level insight in a character's psyche.

- Your task in writing an interior monologue is not only to reveal the person's thoughts and feelings, but to show your **detailed knowledge** and understanding of a given text! As a consequence, you should
  - include relevant information of the plot,
  - explain the situation in which the monologue is held,
  - fill the gap by making explicit what has remained unsaid.

- In the construction of the interior monologue you enjoy a greater stylistic freedom than in writing other texts. However, a good monologue makes use of some of the below listed strategies:
  - **stream of consciousness:** seemingly uncontrolled flow of thoughts; in its extreme form without any punctuation;
  - **rhetorical questions** to show self-doubt or the feeling of being at a loss;
  - incomplete sentences (ellipsis) to indicate that the character's thoughts are unable to follow a logical line; the fast-changing sentences may also reflect a troubled psyche;
  - swear words to point out the emotional intensity of the situation;
  - repetitive use of motifs which are typical for the character to make your text sound authentic;
  - copy of the character's phrases you know from the text, as there presumably is a close relation between a character's language and his/her thoughts.

Dialogue

- Dialogues usually occur in a scene of a play, an interview or as part of a narrative.

- Writing a scene
  - Your task might be that two characters meet in a particular moment (which they do not do in the original play).
  - You should show detailed knowledge of the original by referring to previous actions, meetings etc (although on a real stage this would not happen).
  - Try and copy the **language** of the characters in your scene (e.g. particular phrases, typical sentence structures such as exclamations).
  - Use **stage directions** to indicate what a character does and how he/she says something.

- Making up an interview
  - An interview is set in a particular context you should be aware of. Most likely you – as a German – will talk to an English speaker.
  - Introduce the participants directly or indirectly (e.g.: "Hello, I am Max from Hölderlin-Gymnasium in Stuttgart, thank you for your time, Mr. Ross").
  - Follow the rules of an interview by asking questions which should be answered by your interview partner.
  - Allow misunderstandings and corrections.
  - Pay attention to the different cultural backgrounds (e.g.: "Sorry, I did not understand what you meant by …" / "Can you give me an example for that?").
  - Finish by expressing thanks to your interview partner.

Speech

- Speeches are held in a certain context so that in composing a speech you should be aware of
  - the general historical or cultural setting,
  - the concrete situation (i.e. place and time),
  - your addressees,
  - the purpose of your speech.

- Writing strategies include a surprising opening of your speech, the addressing of the audience and the use of rhetorical devices.

- Do not bore your audience with an opening sentence like "Today I would like to talk about … ." Surprise them by
  - a joke,
  - a quote,
  - a little narrative.

- Address the audience by
  - repetitively referring to your listeners ("Ladies and Gentlemen"),
  - creating a sense of community ("we").

- Use rhetorical devices like professionals, e.g.
  - rhetorical questions,
  - imagery,
  - anaphora (i.e. repetition of the same word or phrase at the beginning of successive clauses).

- Quote or refer to famous people (e.g. politicians, writers), documents (e.g. the Constitution of the United States) or well-known events.

Comparing Characters, Themes and Plots

- A comparison is always based on **criteria** which you have to set up. It is not sufficient to describe e.g. one character and simply add the portrait of another one.

- Criteria for comparing characters might be
  - age,
  - education and profession,
  - character traits such as being egoistic, self-confident, melancholic etc,
  - relation to other characters / to wife or husband / to women or men in general,
  - political or social attitude,
  - the question of being self-determined or driven by circumstances.

- Themes can be compared with respect to
  - their overall importance to the text,
  - their interaction with motifs or other themes.

- When you compare novels or short stories, try and relate the
  - historical, political or social contexts,
  - beginnings,
  - conflicts which arise,
  - endings,
  - characters,
  - themes and motifs,
  - authors' messages.

- Work out **similarities and differences**!

Review

- A review of a film or book consists of
  - a brief summary of the plot,
  - special features of the reviewed piece of art,
  - a personal judgement or recommendation.

- Summary:
  - Do not give too much away, in particular leave the ending open.
  - Mention the most important characters only.
  - Describe what the film or narrative is about (e.g. love, prejudices, multiculturalism).

- Concerning special features in a film, you may comment on
  - costumes,
  - lighting,
  - camera effects,
  - music,
  - actors and their performance.

- For a book review, you could refer to
  - the narrative style,
  - the tradition in which the text stands and the way it differs from others,
  - (post)modern elements,
  - the text's relevance to contemporary issues.

- Overall personal judgement:
  - Base your final (positive or negative) criticism on criteria.
  - Be explicit and clear whether you liked or did not like the piece of art, avoid taking an in-between position.

Mediation

- Mediation is not a simple translation!
- In a mediation you should
  - be aware of the context,
  - briefly characterize the given source for your partner,
  - filter information from the given text,
  - bridge the cultural gap by adding some explanation.
- Context
  - You are usually given a particular context, e.g. as an exchange student in the USA you attend a course on "freedom and security". After the attacks in Paris you might be invited to present the German point of view.
  - This context triggers a particular sort of text (e.g. presentation, blog, introductory speech for a discussion panel).
- Briefly characterize your source. It might be quite a difference whether it is based on the *FAZ* or the *Bild-Zeitung*.
- Filtering
  - Cross out all information which is irrelevant for the given context.
  - Your abstract should be about **half as long** as the given text!
- Mind the cultural gap!
  - German political, cultural or social attitudes might differ very strongly from the ones your partner is used to.
  - In order to avoid confusion, you should give relevant background information.
  - Do not be offensive, rather soften the language and content of the given text if it is necessary.